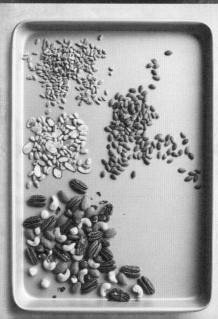
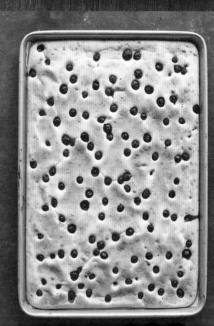

T0356735

SHEET PAN
EVERYTHING

RICARDO

Library and Archives Canada Cataloguing in Publication is available upon request.
ISBN: 9780525610519
eBook ISBN: 9780525610526

THE RICARDO TEAM
Author: Ricardo
Recipe Development: Lisa Birri, Nicolas Cadrin, Kareen Grondin and Etienne Marquis
Recipe Development Contributors: Marc Maula, Éliza Prévost, Antoine Côté-Robitaille and Stéphanie Tremblay
Recipe Tester: Danielle Bessette
Content Director: Maude Bourcier-Bouchard
Art Director: Cristine Berthiaume
Photographer: Maude Chauvin
Designer: Geneviève Larocque
Food Stylists: Etienne Marquis and Nataly Simard
Accessories Stylist: Sylvain Riel
Assistant Photographer: Alma Kismic
Photo Retouching: Jean-Michel Poirier
Graphic Artists: Linda Gravel and Michèle Hénen
Editor: Marie-Pier Gagnon
Translation: Joanna Fox and Michelle Diamond
Translation revision: Katie Moore
Project Manager - Kitchen: Eve Marchand
Production Coordinator: Marisol Moquin Laferrière

President and Editorial Director: Brigitte Coutu
Vice-President Communications and Brand Image: Nathalie Carbonneau

ricardocuisine.com

Printed and bound in China

Published in Canada by Appetite by Random House®,
a division of Penguin Random House Canada Limited.

www.penguinrandomhouse.ca

10 9 8 7 6 5 4

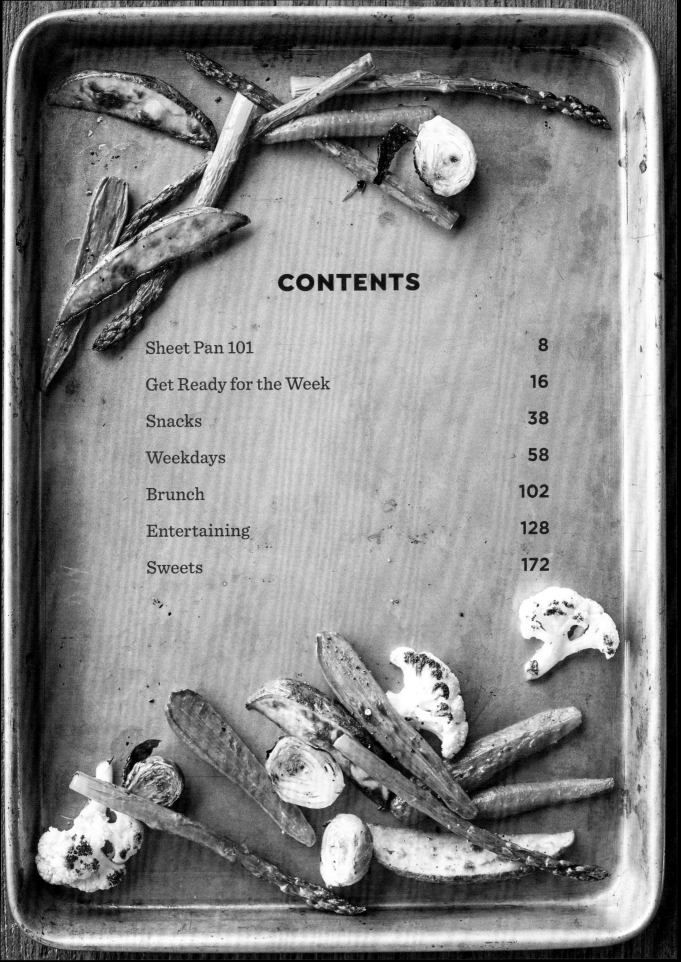

CONTENTS

YOUR
NEW ALLY

Buried in your oven drawer or stacked in a kitchen cupboard, you may have a stained and well-worn sheet pan that's seen you through hundreds of meals, or maybe you have one that's brand new and barely been used. If you're holding this book in your hands right now, I guarantee that if you have a sheet pan, you'll use it now, more than ever.

You probably bought a sheet pan for the first time to bake cookies, make frozen French fries or roast vegetables. In this book, I want to take it a step further, going beyond cooking a single ingredient and using the sheet pan to its full capacity: making a complete meal. In the development of this book, my kitchen team and I tried to cook *everything* on a sheet pan, with the exception of most pastas, rice and some grains (trust us, they just don't work).

Cooking on a sheet pan is simple, it concentrates flavors, it requires little handling and it has virtually no messy cleanup. In contrast to the slow cooker, sheet pan meals have the advantage of speed. The metal of the pan can withstand high temperatures and allows for broiling, so you can finish your dish under the broiler for a few minutes for even more caramelization.

But the best part about cooking with a sheet pan? It combines what we love to celebrate in the kitchen: simplicity and togetherness. When you place the pan in the center of the table, everyone instantly relaxes, gathers around and talks about their day. And it's also a serious time-saver, as it takes only a few minutes to toss together the ingredients for a full and balanced meal—giving you more time to enjoy with your loved ones.

When we started creating these recipes, our world was a totally different place. We were always crowded around various sheet pan dishes together in the test kitchen, offering each other suggestions and pushing ourselves further to get the recipes just right. When we finished them, we were isolated from one another, working from our respective homes. But eating these recipes again, with our families during confinement, we realized they were exactly what we needed.

With this book, my wish is to help everyone have soothing, satisfying and comforting moments around the table.

Bon appétit!

SHEET PAN 101

DIMENSIONS

A standard sheet pan usually measures 18 × 13 inches (46 × 33 cm). There are also small sheet pans, often referred to as quarter sheet pans in professional kitchens, that measure 13 × 9 inches (33 × 23 cm). These smaller sheets can be practical when making desserts or roasting a smaller quantity of vegetables, for example.

COOKIE SHEET VS. SHEET PAN

The difference between a cookie sheet (or pastry sheet) and a sheet pan is the absence of raised sides on a cookie sheet. Some cookie sheets do have one raised side, which helps to easily slide food off the sheet. I only use sheet pans with raised sides because they hold in cooking juices and are more durable and less likely to warp over time.

PALE VS. DARK SHEET PAN

Some sheet pans are dark while others are pale. A dark sheet will absorb more of the oven's radiant heat, which can then overly brown and caramelize the foods cooked on it. A pale sheet reflects heat and encourages more even cooking. For example, if you bake cookies on a dark sheet pan, they will brown much more quickly and could even burn! You can reduce the cooking time by a few minutes in this case.

A non-stick sheet pan is easy to maintain because foods will not stick to it as they cook.

An aluminum sheet pan is light and versatile but does not age well over time. Also, the aluminum may react with acidic foods, damaging the sheet.

A textured sheet pan prevents foods from sticking to it.

An enameled cast-iron sheet pan is usually colored and has a very thick bottom. If using one, you will likely have to run a few tests first and possibly increase the cooking time of your recipes.

GOOD TO KNOW

All of the recipes in this book were tested with RICARDO brand non-stick sheet pans. These fall under the category of *pale* sheet pans. Unless otherwise indicated in the recipe, we used a standard 18 × 13-inch (46 × 33 cm) sheet pan.

CHOOSING THE RIGHT LINING

Aluminum foil is perfect for cooking at very high temperatures, especially when broiling. It is also practical when using spices that could stain your sheet pan.

A silicone mat can be reused again and again over a long period. It is not recommended for use under the broiler or at temperatures above 425°F (220°C), which could cause it to deteriorate.

Parchment paper
You should avoid putting parchment paper under the broiler, as it may burn. Some cities will allow you to compost parchment paper after it has been used, but it is best to check local composting rules before doing so.

Avoid using wax paper, which tends to burn and stick to foods. We recommend not using parchment paper or a silicone mat for a recipe with sauce since the sauce could seep under the paper. For those recipes, use an unlined, non-stick sheet pan.

GOOD TO KNOW

When you have several sheet pans in the oven at once, cook on convection, if you have it, to encourage even cooking. Cutting your ingredients into uniform pieces will also ensure even cooking.

OVEN TEMPERATURE

To get nice browning on your vegetables and a good sear on your meats without burning anything onto your sheet pan, the ideal oven temperature is 425°F (220°C). If you are ever stuck wondering what temperature to set your oven at for sheet pan cooking, this is a good place to start.

PLACING THE OVEN RACKS

We have been careful to indicate in each recipe where to place your rack in the oven. Be sure to place your sheet pan on the center of the rack to encourage good heat circulation.

CARE INSTRUCTIONS

Eventually all sheet pans will become stained. It's frustrating but unavoidable and totally normal. These stains will not compromise the quality of your sheet pan.

If your sheet pan does become badly stained, wash it before putting it back in the oven. If you re-cook a stain, it will be stuck there forever! When washing off those stubborn stains before they set in, remember that non-stick and enameled cast-iron sheet pans are dishwasher-safe, while aluminum sheets are not (over time they will become damaged by the dishwasher soap). It is better to let them soak in water before washing them by hand.

IN ADDITION

Never cut directly on a sheet pan with a knife or pizza cutter, especially if it is non-stick. The same goes for silicone mats. For stirring and serving, use nylon, wood or silicone utensils.

WHEN A SHEET PAN GOES "BOOM"

Has your heart ever skipped a beat after hearing a sheet pan twist loudly in the oven? Don't worry! This phenomenon is not due to shoddy equipment, but rather is a result of thermal shock. Your sheet pan will return to its original shape once cooled.

NOTES
FROM RICARDO AND TEAM

IT WASN'T ALWAYS EASY!

While cooking on sheet pans will simplify your life at home, it really complicated the lives of our recipe developers. For each recipe in this book, we had to make sure that the dish not only worked being cooked on a sheet pan but was actually enhanced by this cooking method. Cooking on sheet pans became a complicated math problem that wasn't always easy to solve! Sometimes the recipe was too large to fit on one sheet pan, but using two sheets didn't deliver the best results either. After all of our testing, we encourage you to follow our tips and recommendations within the recipes for best results.

NOT ALL OVENS ARE CREATED EQUAL.

Every oven is different, so you have to be attentive and adaptable. It is only after making a recipe several times that you finally get the best results. We tested the recipes in this book in different ovens, so consider the oven temperatures and cooking times as guidelines and not absolutes. Try changing the position of your oven racks or cooking on convection for better browning. It's not an exact science!

LESS IS MORE.

Do not be tempted to overload your sheet pan. Your food will steam rather than brown up nicely. We purposely space out the ingredients on our sheets, even when adding a starchy side, as with the noodles in our glazed tofu, edamame and vermicelli bowl (p. 80). For maximum caramelization, you can always finish off cooking under the broiler.

NOT EVERY RECIPE BENEFITS FROM THE SHEET PAN TREATMENT.

We wouldn't be doing you any favors if we adapted all of your favorite recipes for the sheet pan method. The sky was not the limit with this project. We did attempt to cook rice, grains and various other dishes on a sheet pan—with disastrous results! Rest assured that you will have nothing but success with the recipes that made it into this book.

I WOULD HAVE LIKED MORE SAUCE WITH THAT!

Everyone likes sauce (us included!), but having too much can result in the sheet pan overflowing or your food taking a steam bath. Too much liquid creates too much steam and prevents your food from nicely browning. Your food will be cooked, yes, but will not caramelize. For recipes that call for sauce, we opt to make it separately in a pot.

NOT EVERYTHING ON MY SHEET PAN IS PERFECTLY BROWNED!

That's totally normal! With sheet pan cooking, not all of your ingredients will be uniformly browned. For example, a piece of white chicken without any added fat or sweet sauce will not brown. Use this to your advantage, as we did with our recipe for warm Greek chicken salad (p. 60), where the chicken emerges from the oven perfectly tender and juicy.

roasted tomato
and garlic sauce

SHEET PAN
MEAL PREP

A little sheet pan prep on the weekend will help you throw together your weekday meals with ease. Some of these essentials are used throughout the cookbook, but also work wonders on their own!

vegetarian lentil "meatballs"

ROASTED EGGPLANT

1	large eggplant, cut into 1/2-inch (1 cm) rounds
3 tbsp	(45 ml) olive oil

With the rack in the middle position, preheat the oven to 425°F (220°C). Line a sheet pan with a silicone mat or parchment paper.

On the sheet pan, toss the eggplant slices with the oil. Season with salt and pepper. Arrange the eggplant in a single layer, making sure the slices do not overlap. Bake for 20 to 25 minutes or until nicely roasted, turning over halfway through. The eggplant rounds will keep for 5 days in an airtight container at room temperature.

PREPARATION
5 MIN

COOKING
20 MIN

MAKES
1 1/2 CUPS (375 ML), APPROX.

FREEZES
YES

ROASTED BELL PEPPERS

6	bell peppers, various colors, halved and seeded
2 tbsp	(30 ml) vegetable oil

With the rack in the middle position, preheat the oven to 450°F (230°C).

On a non-stick or parchment paper–lined sheet pan, coat the bell peppers in the oil. Place skin-side up. Season with salt and pepper. Bake for 30 minutes or until tender and slightly charred. Place in an airtight container and let cool for 20 minutes. Remove the skin. The roasted bell peppers will keep for 2 weeks in an airtight container in the refrigerator.

PREPARATION
20 MIN

COOKING
30 MIN

COOLING
20 MIN

FREEZES
YES

MAKES
3 CUPS (750 ML), APPROX.

CARAMELIZED ONIONS

8 cups	(1 kg) onions, cut into very thin wedges (6 medium onions)
1/4 cup	(60 ml) olive oil
2 tbsp	(30 ml) sherry vinegar or balsamic vinegar
2	sprigs thyme

With the rack in the middle position, preheat the oven to 425°F (220°C). Line a sheet pan with a silicone mat or parchment paper.

On the sheet pan, toss all of the ingredients together. Season with salt and pepper.

Bake for 55 minutes or until the onions are nicely browned, stirring a few times during cooking.

These are delicious as a topping for sandwiches or in our crispy ham and cheese wrap (recipe p. 110). The caramelized onions will keep for 1 week in an airtight container in the refrigerator.

PREPARATION	COOKING	MAKES	FREEZES
20 MIN	55 MIN	2 CUPS (500 ML)	YES

chili
seasoning

sesame
seasoning

lime
seasoning

PITA CHIPS

5	pita breads (about 7 inches/18 cm in diameter)
2 tbsp	(30 ml) olive oil
1	seasoning of your choice (below)

SESAME SEASONING	LIME SEASONING	CHILI SEASONING
1 tbsp sesame seeds	1 tsp ground cumin	1 tsp chili powder
1 tsp ground sumac	1/2 tsp onion salt	1/2 tsp onion salt
1/4 tsp salt	1/4 tsp ground black pepper	1/2 tsp garlic powder
	1 lime, zest finely grated	1/4 tsp ground black pepper

With the rack in the middle position, preheat the oven to 350°F (180°C).

On a work surface, using a chef's knife or kitchen scissors, cut each pita into eight triangles.

In a large bowl, combine the oil with the seasoning of your choice. Add the pita triangles to the bowl and toss to coat well with the seasoning. Spread out on a non-stick sheet pan (the pitas will be slightly overlapping).

Bake for 10 to 12 minutes or until golden and crispy, turning the chips over halfway through.

These are delicious served with a dip or crumbled into a salad. The pita chips will keep for 2 weeks in an airtight container at room temperature.

PREPARATION	COOKING	MAKES	FREEZES
15 MIN	10 MIN	40 CHIPS	–

TOASTED COUSCOUS

3 cups (600 g) medium couscous, uncooked

With the rack in the middle position, preheat a convection oven to 425°F (220°C) (see note).

Spread the couscous out directly on a non-stick sheet pan. Bake for 15 to 20 minutes or until golden, stirring two or three times during cooking. Let cool. The toasted couscous will keep for 3 months in an airtight container at room temperature.

NOTE *Cooking the couscous on convection helps the grains cook more evenly. If using a conventional oven, stir more often during cooking.*

PREPARATION	COOKING	MAKES	FREEZES
2 MIN	15 MIN	3 CUPS (600 G)	–

ONE OF OUR READERS REACHED
OUT TO TELL ME ABOUT
TOASTING COUSCOUS PRIOR TO
COOKING FOR ENHANCED FLAVOR.
I THOUGHT IT WAS SUCH A SMART IDEA,
I PUT IT IN MY BOOK!

BACON AND PANCETTA

Place bacon or pancetta slices on a sheet pan lined with parchment paper. With the rack in the middle position, bake in the oven at the temperature indicated. Once cooked, pat down with paper towel. The cooked bacon and pancetta will keep for 2 weeks in an airtight container in the refrigerator. When ready to use, reheat in a skillet or microwave oven.

NOT ONLY DOES THIS BACON STAY STRAIGHT AND FLAT, IT ALSO DOESN'T SPLATTER THE COUNTERTOP!

15 MIN
at 400°F (200°C)

10 MIN
at 350°F (180°C)

PARMESAN AND ALMOND TUILES

1/2 cup	**(35 g) freshly grated Parmesan cheese**
2 tbsp	**sliced almonds**

With the rack in the middle position, preheat the oven to 375°F (190°C). Line a sheet pan with a silicone mat or parchment paper.

For each tuile, place 1 tbsp of Parmesan on the sheet pan and spread out to a 3-inch (7.5 cm) circle, using the back of a spoon or your fingers. Sprinkle with the almonds. Season lightly with pepper.

Bake for 8 minutes or until the cheese is melted and slightly golden. Let cool on the sheet pan. The Parmesan tuiles will keep for 1 week in an airtight container at room temperature.

NOTE *You can easily omit the almonds.*

PREPARATION	COOKING	MAKES	FREEZES
10 MIN	8 MIN	8 TUILES	–

\ | / ,

I ALWAYS HAVE THESE TWO INGREDIENTS ON HAND, READY TO ACCOMPANY IMPROMPTU DRINKS!

/ / | \ `

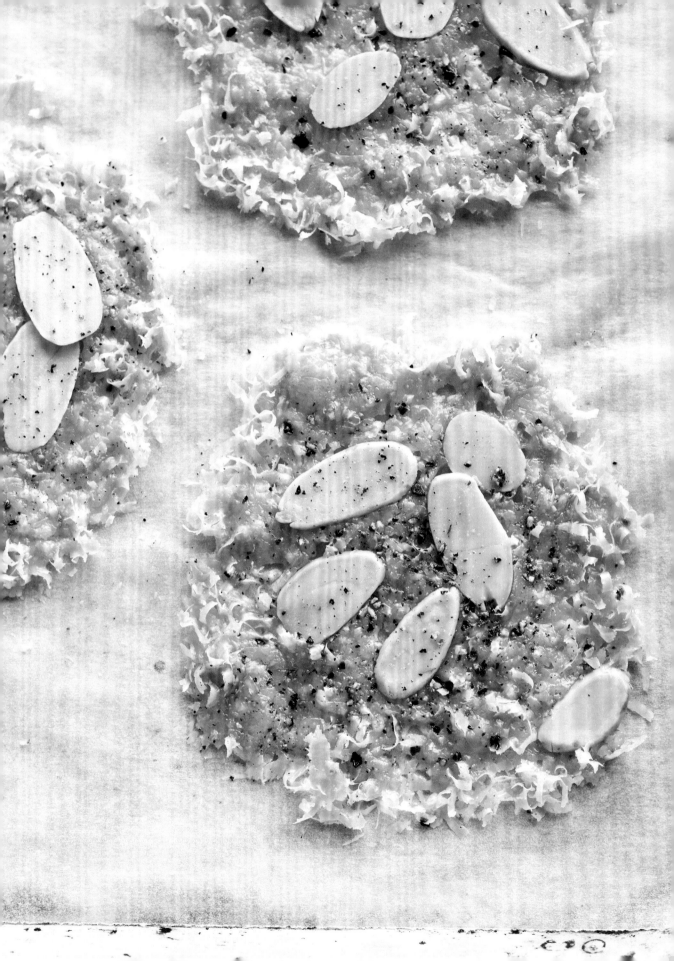

ROASTED NUTS AND SEEDS

Place the nuts and seeds directly on the sheet pan. Bake at 350°F (180°C), stirring halfway through cooking. The nuts and seeds will keep for 3 weeks in an airtight container at room temperature.

NOTE *Some nuts will split open slightly when ready, such as almonds and hazelnuts.*

10 TO 12 MIN
pecans, walnuts, hazelnuts, whole almonds and cashews

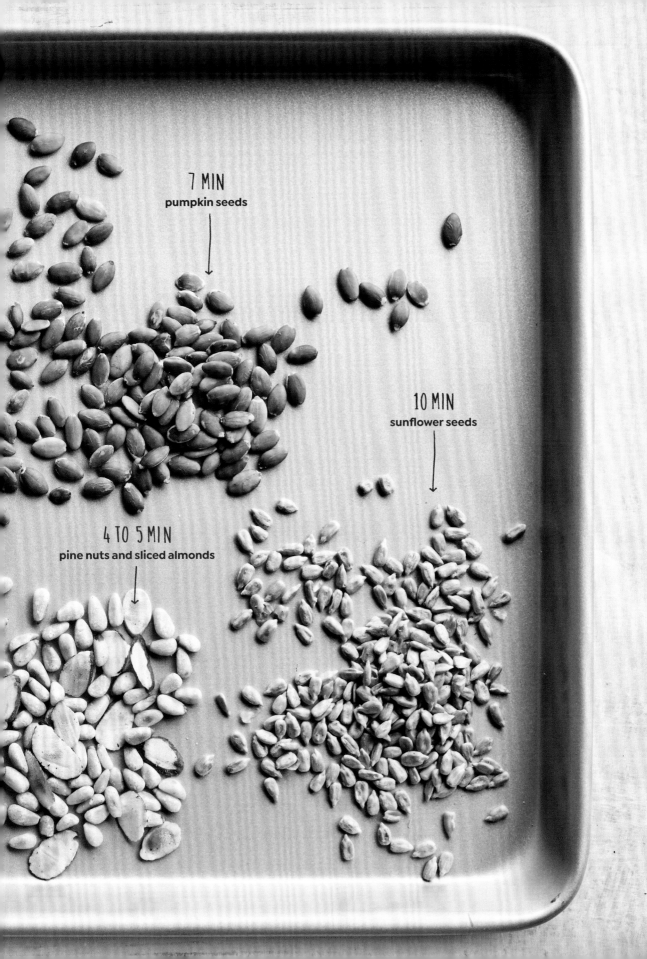

7 MIN
pumpkin seeds

10 MIN
sunflower seeds

4 TO 5 MIN
pine nuts and sliced almonds

ROASTED TOMATO AND GARLIC SAUCE

3 1/2 lb   (1.6 kg) plum tomatoes, cored and halved (about 12 tomatoes)
3   large garlic cloves, unpeeled
1/4 cup   (60 ml) olive oil
1/4 tsp   red pepper flakes

With the rack in the middle position, preheat a convection oven to 425°F (220°C) (see note).

On a non-stick sheet pan, toss all of the ingredients together. Season with salt and pepper. Arrange the tomatoes cut-side down. Bake for 50 minutes to 1 hour or until the tomatoes are nicely roasted. Let cool.

With your fingers, peel the tomatoes and garlic. Compost or discard the peels.

In a food processor, pulse all of the ingredients for a few seconds at a time until smooth. The sauce will keep for 1 week in an airtight container in the refrigerator.

NOTE *Cooking on convection allows for more of the liquid to evaporate. If cooking in a conventional oven, the cooking time will be longer.*

PREPARATION	COOKING	MAKES	FREEZES
10 MIN	50 MIN	2 CUPS (500 ML), APPROX.	YES

VEGETARIAN LENTIL "MEATBALLS"

1/4 cup (60 ml) vegetable oil
2 cups (260 g) grated zucchini (2 small zucchini)
2 cans (14 oz/398 ml each) brown lentils, rinsed and drained
2 green onions, chopped
1 cup (100 g) grated mozzarella cheese
1 cup (70 g) freshly grated Parmesan cheese
2 eggs
1/4 cup (30 g) breadcrumbs
1/4 cup (30 g) ground chia seeds
1/2 tsp garlic powder

With the rack in the middle position, preheat the oven to 400°F (200°C). Grease a non-stick sheet pan with the oil.

Place the grated zucchini in a clean dishcloth and squeeze out as much liquid as possible. Place the zucchini in a food processor.

Add the lentils and green onions. Purée until relatively smooth. Transfer to a bowl. Add both cheeses, the eggs, breadcrumbs, ground chia seeds and garlic powder. Season with salt and pepper. Mix well.

Using a 1 tbsp (15 ml) ice cream scoop, form the mixture into balls and finish rolling with lightly oiled hands. Place the balls on the sheet pan, coating them in the oil.

Bake for 20 minutes, turning the balls over halfway through. Serve as an appetizer, with pasta and tomato sauce or in a pita sandwich. The vegetarian "meatballs" will keep for 5 days in an airtight container in the refrigerator.

PREPARATION	COOKING	MAKES	FREEZES
35 MIN	20 MIN	65 MEATBALLS, APPROX.	YES

I'M CRAZY ABOUT MEATBALLS.
I PUT THEM IN EVERYTHING!
THESE ONES ARE GREAT SERVED
WITH HUMMUS.

BEEF AND LAMB MEATBALLS

1	egg
1/4 cup	(60 ml) milk
1/2 cup	(65 g) breadcrumbs
3/4 lb	(340 g) lean ground beef (see note)
3/4 lb	(340 g) ground lamb
1/2 tsp	ground cumin

With the rack in the middle position, preheat the oven to 425°F (220°C). Line a sheet pan with a silicone mat or parchment paper.

In a large bowl, combine the egg, milk and breadcrumbs. Add the remaining ingredients and mix well with your hands. Season with salt and pepper.

Using a 1 tbsp (15 ml) ice cream scoop, form the mixture into balls and finish rolling with lightly oiled hands. Place the meatballs on the sheet pan.

Bake for 12 to 15 minutes or until the meatballs are cooked through and lightly browned.

Serve as an appetizer, in a soup or in pasta sauce. These meatballs are a great addition to a pita sandwich along with lettuce, red onion, cucumber and tzatziki. The meatballs will keep for 5 days in an airtight container in the refrigerator.

NOTE *The meatballs can be made with 1 1/2 lb (675 g) ground lamb only, but for a milder-tasting and less expensive version, we opted for equal amounts of ground lamb and beef.*

PREPARATION	COOKING	MAKES	FREEZES
20 MIN	12 MIN	50 MEATBALLS, APPROX.	YES

ranch chickpea snack

fruit rollups

sweet and salty
maple nuts

SHEET PAN
SNACKS

Get ready to satisfy those little cravings!

barbecue party mix

bran, banana
and raisin muffins

SWEET AND SALTY MAPLE NUTS

1	egg white
2 cups	(265 g) unsalted nuts (such as almonds, cashews, pecans)
1/4 cup	(40 g) maple sugar
1 tsp	fleur de sel

With the rack in the middle position, preheat the oven to 350°F (180°C). Line a sheet pan with a silicone mat or parchment paper.

In a bowl, whisk the egg white until soft peaks form. Add the nuts, maple sugar and fleur de sel. Mix well. Spread out on the sheet pan.

Bake for 25 minutes or until the nuts are nicely browned, stirring twice during cooking. Let cool completely. The nuts will keep for 2 months in an airtight container at room temperature.

PREPARATION	COOKING	MAKES	FREEZES
10 MIN	25 MIN	2 CUPS (500 ML)	–

FRUIT ROLLUPS

2 cups   **(250 g) frozen berries, thawed (such as raspberries, blueberries, blackberries or strawberries)**
1 cup   **(250 ml) unsweetened applesauce**
2 tbsp **sugar**

With the rack in the middle position, preheat the oven to 170°F (75°C). Line a sheet pan with a silicone mat (see note).

In a blender, purée all of the ingredients until smooth. Strain through a sieve. Spread the mixture out evenly on the sheet pan using an offset spatula. Tap the sheet pan on the counter to help even out the mixture.

Bake for 3 to 4 hours, opening the oven door twice during cooking to release steam, until the fruit paste is dry to the touch. Let cool.

Using kitchen scissors, cut the fruit paste into 1-inch (2.5 cm) wide strips and roll up. The fruit rollups will keep for 1 month in an airtight container at room temperature.

NOTE *We prefer using a silicone mat rather than parchment paper for this recipe to encourage the water from the fruit to evaporate more quickly. It is important to use a straight-sided, non-warped sheet pan to ensure even cooking. If the sheet pan is warped, parts of the fruit paste will be overcooked while other parts will be undercooked. If your oven does not go as low as 170°F (75°C), you can cook this recipe at 200°F (95°C) and reduce the cooking time to between 2 1/2 and 3 hours.*

PREPARATION	COOKING	MAKES	FREEZES
10 MIN	3 H	15 ROLLUPS	–

LET THE KIDS
LEND A HAND!

PECAN GRANOLA

1/2 cup	(115 g) unsalted butter, melted
1/2 cup	(105 g) brown sugar
4 cups	(400 g) large oat flakes
2 cups	(200 g) coarsely chopped pecans
2 tbsp	sesame seeds
1	egg white

With the rack in the middle position, preheat the oven to 350°F (180°C). Line a sheet pan with a silicone mat or parchment paper.

In a bowl, combine the butter and brown sugar. Add the oats, pecans and sesame seeds. Mix well.

In another bowl, whisk the egg white with an electric mixer until frothy. Add the egg white to the oat mixture. Spread out on the sheet pan.

Bake for 30 minutes, stirring every 10 minutes. Let cool completely.

The pecan granola will keep for 1 month in an airtight container at room temperature.

PREPARATION	COOKING	MAKES	FREEZES
15 MIN	30 MIN	8 CUPS (2 L), APPROX.	—

BARBECUE PARTY MIX

1/4 cup   (55 g) butter, melted
1 tbsp   (15 ml) Worcestershire sauce
1 tbsp   chili powder
1 tsp   (5 ml) Tabasco-style sauce
4 cups   (120 g) toasted rice, corn or wheat cereal (Chex-style)
2 cups   (265 g) mixed nuts (such as almonds, cashews, pecans)

With the rack in the middle position, preheat the oven to 250°F (120°C). Line a sheet pan with a silicone mat or parchment paper.

In a large bowl, combine the butter, Worcestershire sauce, chili powder and Tabasco-style sauce. Add the cereal and nuts. Stir to coat well in the butter mixture. Spread out on the sheet pan.

Bake for 1 hour, stirring twice during cooking. Let cool completely. The party mix will keep for 1 month in an airtight container at room temperature.

PREPARATION	COOKING	MAKES	FREEZES
10 MIN	1 H	6 CUPS (1.5 L)	–

FROZEN YOGURT BARK

4 oz (115 g) white chocolate, chopped
2 cups (500 ml) 5% plain Greek yogurt, at room temperature
3 oz (85 g) 70% dark chocolate, chopped
1/2 cup (75 g) dried cranberries, chopped
1/4 cup (35 g) roasted shelled pistachios, chopped

Line a sheet pan with a silicone mat or parchment paper.

In a bowl, over a double boiler or in a microwave oven, melt the white chocolate.

Add the yogurt and whisk until smooth.

Spread out evenly on the sheet pan. Sprinkle with the dark chocolate, cranberries and pistachios. Gently press the toppings into the yogurt mixture. Freeze for 2 hours.

Break into pieces and serve. The frozen yogurt bark will keep for 3 months in an airtight container in the freezer.

PREPARATION	COOKING	FREEZING	SERVINGS	FREEZES
15 MIN	5 MIN	2 H	12	REQUIRED

SHEET PANS ARE ALSO
FREEZER-FRIENDLY!

THE DREAM:
MUFFIN TOPS
FOR DAYS!

BRAN, BANANA AND RAISIN MUFFINS

1 1/2 cups	(225 g) unbleached all-purpose flour
1 1/2 cups	(90 g) wheat bran
1 tsp	baking powder
1/2 tsp	baking soda
3/4 cup	(160 g) brown sugar
3/4 cup	(180 ml) buttermilk (see note)
1/2 cup	(125 ml) canola oil
2	eggs
1	very ripe banana, mashed with a fork
1/2 cup	(70 g) raisins, plus more to garnish

With the rack in the middle position, preheat the oven to 375°F (190°C). Line a small 13 × 9-inch (33 × 23 cm) sheet pan with parchment paper, letting it hang over two sides.

In a bowl, combine the flour, wheat bran, baking powder and baking soda.

In another bowl, whisk together the brown sugar, buttermilk, oil, eggs and banana. Add the dry ingredients. Stir with a spatula just until the dry ingredients are moistened. Add the raisins. Spread the mixture out on the sheet pan. Sprinkle with a few more raisins.

Bake for 18 to 20 minutes or until a toothpick inserted in the center of the muffin comes out clean. Let cool completely on a wire rack. Cut into squares or bars. The muffins will keep for 3 to 4 days in an airtight container at room temperature.

NOTE *If you do not have buttermilk, make your own by adding 1 tbsp (15 ml) white vinegar or lemon juice to 3/4 cup (180 ml) milk. Let sit for 5 minutes. Stir before using.*

PREPARATION	**COOKING**	**MAKES**	**FREEZES**
15 MIN	18 MIN	12 SQUARES	YES

DRIED APPLES

5	Cortland apples, peeled, seeded and each cut into 16 thin wedges

With both racks in the middle positions, preheat the oven to 170°F (75°C). Line two sheet pans with parchment paper (see note).

Spread the apples out on the sheet pans without letting the slices touch.

Bake for 6 hours or until dry but still pliable. Let cool completely. The dried apples will keep for 1 week in an airtight container at room temperature or for several months in the freezer. They are delicious directly from the freezer.

NOTE *You can bake the apples directly on the sheet pan with no parchment paper, but the apples will be crispier and less tender. If your oven does not go as low as 170°F (75°C), you can cook this recipe at 200°F (95°C) and reduce the cooking time to 3 to 4 hours.*

PREPARATION	COOKING	MAKES	FREEZES
15 MIN	6 H	3 CUPS (750 ML), APPROX.	YES

HONEY AND APRICOT GRANOLA BARS

4 cups	**(400 g) large oat flakes**
1 cup	**(130 g) unsalted cashews (see note)**
1 cup	**(160 g) dried apricots, cut into pieces**
1/2 cup	**(125 ml) orange juice**
1/2 cup	**(125 ml) almond butter, at room temperature**
1/2 cup	**(125 ml) honey**
1/4 cup	**(60 ml) vegetable oil**
1 cup	**(70 g) shredded unsweetened coconut**
1 cup	**(30 g) puffed quinoa**

With the rack in the middle position, preheat the oven to 350°F (180°C). Line a sheet pan with parchment paper (see note).

Spread the oats and nuts out on the sheet pan. Bake for 15 minutes or until slightly golden, stirring halfway through. Let cool. Reduce the oven temperature to 300°F (150°C).

In a food processor, purée the apricots and orange juice until smooth. Transfer to a large bowl.

Add the almond butter, honey and oil to the bowl. Mix well. Add the cooled oats and nuts, coconut and puffed quinoa. Stir until moistened. Spread out evenly on the sheet pan, pressing down firmly with the bottom of a glass.

Bake for 30 minutes or until nicely browned.

Let cool completely. Cut into bars. The granola bars will keep for 2 weeks in an airtight container at room temperature, the layers separated with pieces of parchment paper.

NOTES *The cashews can be replaced with nuts of your choice.*

Use parchment paper for this recipe since we are cutting the bars directly on the sheet pan (cutting on a silicone mat will damage it).

PREPARATION	COOKING	MAKES	FREEZES
25 MIN	45 MIN	30 BARS	YES

RANCH CHICKPEA SNACK

2 cans   (19 oz/540 ml each) chickpeas, rinsed and drained
3 tbsp   (45 ml) vegetable oil
RANCH SPICE
1 tsp   dried parsley
1/2 tsp   dried oregano
1/2 tsp   celery salt
1/2 tsp   dry mustard
1/2 tsp   onion powder
1/4 tsp   garlic powder

With the rack in the middle position, preheat the oven to 400°F (200°C).

On a work surface, rub the chickpeas between two clean dishcloths to remove the skins and to pat dry.

On a non-stick sheet pan, combine the dried chickpeas with the oil. Bake for 50 minutes or until the chickpeas are golden and have cracked open, stirring every 10 minutes.

RANCH SPICE
Meanwhile, in a small bowl, combine all of the spices.

When the chickpeas are ready, toss with the spices. Season with salt and pepper. Let cool completely.

The ranch chickpeas will keep for a few days in an airtight container at room temperature (see note).

NOTE *If your ranch chickpeas start to soften, place them directly on a non-stick sheet pan and bake for a few minutes at 325°F (165°C) to crisp them up.*

PREPARATION	COOKING	MAKES	FREEZES
15 MIN	50 MIN	2 CUPS (500 ML), APPROX.	–

glazed tofu, edamame
and vermicelli bowl

SHEET PAN
WEEKDAYS

*Move over, slow cooker, the sheet pan
is your new weekday dinner partner!*

WARM GREEK CHICKEN SALAD

DRESSING

1/4 cup	(60 ml) olive oil
3 tbsp	(45 ml) lemon juice
1 tbsp	(15 ml) honey
1 tsp	dried oregano
2	garlic cloves, finely chopped

SALAD

1 1/2 lb	(675 g) boneless, skinless chicken breasts (about 3 breasts)
2 cups	(280 g) cherry tomatoes
1/4 cup	(50 g) pitted kalamata olives, cut into rounds
1	red onion, thinly sliced
7 oz	(200 g) crumbled feta cheese
1/4 cup	(10 g) flat-leaf parsley
4	Lebanese cucumbers, cut into 1/4-inch (6 mm) rounds
2	romaine lettuce hearts, torn

DRESSING

In a large bowl, whisk together all of the ingredients. Season with salt and pepper.

SALAD

With the rack in the middle position, preheat the oven to 400°F (200°C). On a non-stick sheet pan, toss the chicken with 2 tbsp (30 ml) of the dressing. Bake for 15 minutes. Set the remaining dressing aside.

Remove the sheet pan from the oven. Arrange the tomatoes, olives and onion (see note) around the chicken. Bake for another 5 minutes or until the chicken is cooked through.

Let cool for 5 minutes. On a work surface, thinly slice the chicken and return to the sheet pan. Adjust the seasoning. Sprinkle with the cheese and parsley.

Add the cucumbers and lettuce to the bowl of dressing. Mix well.

Serve the salad in bowls. Top with the chicken mixture.

NOTE *By adding the onion at this stage, it loses its strong raw onion taste while staying crisp. If desired, you can cook the onion longer by adding it at the same time as the chicken.*

PREPARATION	COOKING	SERVINGS	FREEZES
25 MIN	20 MIN	4	–

THE PERFECT
WARM-COLD COMBO.

CHICKEN WINGS AND CAULIFLOWER WITH HONEY-MUSTARD SAUCE

WINGS AND CAULIFLOWER

12	chicken wings (see note)
2 tsp	baking powder
2 tsp	cornstarch
1/2 tsp	salt
1/2	cauliflower, cut into small florets (5 cups/500 g)
1 tbsp	(15 ml) vegetable oil
	Flat-leaf parsley, finely chopped (optional)

HONEY-MUSTARD SAUCE

1/4 cup	(60 ml) honey
1/4 cup	(60 ml) prepared mustard
2 tbsp	(30 ml) whole-grain mustard
1 tbsp	(15 ml) apple cider vinegar
1 tsp	(5 ml) Tabasco-style sauce

WINGS AND CAULIFLOWER

With the rack in the middle position, preheat the oven to 425°F (220°C). Line a sheet pan with parchment paper.

On a work surface, cut each chicken wing through the joints into three pieces. Compost or discard the wing tips and keep only the two large pieces of each wing. Pat dry with paper towel.

In a large bowl, combine the baking powder, cornstarch and salt. Add the chicken wings and toss to coat well. Lay out on the sheet pan. Bake for 40 minutes.

In another bowl, toss the cauliflower with the oil. Season with salt and pepper.

Flip the wings over and add the cauliflower to the sheet pan. Bake for another 15 minutes or until the wings are golden, the meat falls easily from the bones and the cauliflower is al dente.

HONEY-MUSTARD SAUCE

Meanwhile, in a small pot, bring all of the ingredients to a boil. Simmer for 5 minutes or until the sauce is syrupy. Pour the sauce into a large bowl. Add the chicken wings and cauliflower. Toss to coat well in the sauce. Sprinkle with parsley, if desired. Serve immediately.

NOTE *Chicken wings are sold whole or in pieces. If they are whole, you will need to separate them into pieces as described in the recipe. Regardless of how you buy them, you will need a total of 24 pieces.*

PREPARATION	COOKING	SERVINGS	FREEZES
25 MIN	55 MIN	4	–

BYE-BYE,
DEEP FRYER.

FISH AND CHIPS

1 1/2 lb   (675 g) small baby potatoes, halved
2 tbsp   (30 ml) vegetable oil, plus more for the asparagus
1/2 cup   (125 ml) mayonnaise
1 tsp   (5 ml) harissa
1/2 cup   (40 g) panko breadcrumbs
2 tbsp   butter, melted
1 lb   (450 g) small asparagus, trimmed
1 1/2 lb   (675 g) hake or haddock fillets, cut into 4 pieces
           Lemon wedges, for serving

With the rack in the middle position, preheat the oven to 450°F (230°C).

On a non-stick sheet pan, toss the potatoes with the oil. Season with salt and pepper. Arrange in a single layer, cut-side down. Bake for 20 minutes.

Meanwhile, in a small bowl, combine the mayonnaise and harissa. Set aside.

In another bowl, combine the breadcrumbs and butter. Set aside.

Toss the asparagus with a drizzle of oil.

Remove the sheet pan from the oven. Gently toss the asparagus with the potatoes. Nestle the fish pieces among the vegetables, making sure the bottoms come in direct contact with the sheet pan. Season lightly with salt. Brush the tops of the fish pieces with 1 tbsp (15 ml) of the spicy mayonnaise. Cover the mayonnaise with the breadcrumb mixture and press lightly to adhere.

Bake for 8 to 10 minutes or until the fish is cooked through and the breadcrumbs are slightly golden. Finish off cooking under the broiler, if desired.

Serve the fish and vegetables with the remaining spicy mayonnaise and lemon wedges.

PREPARATION	COOKING	SERVINGS	FREEZES
20 MIN	30 MIN	4	–

CHICKEN LEGS WITH
RED ONIONS AND PARSNIPS

6	whole chicken legs with skin
1 1/2 tsp	salt
1/2	lemon
1 lb	(450 g) parsnips, peeled and halved lengthwise
6	small red onions, peeled and halved
3	garlic cloves, unpeeled and crushed
10 to 12	sage leaves
2 tbsp	(30 ml) olive oil
1/2 tsp	ground black pepper

With the rack in the middle position, preheat the oven to 375°F (190°C). Line a sheet pan with foil (see note p. 10).

On a work surface, season the chicken with the salt and rub all over with the lemon half. Lay the chicken out on the sheet pan, skin-side up.

Squeeze the lemon juice into a large bowl. Add the remaining ingredients and toss to coat the vegetables well. Arrange the mixture around the chicken on the sheet pan, placing the onions cut-side down.

Bake for 1 hour 15 minutes or until the vegetables are tender and the meat falls easily from the bones, turning the parsnips over halfway through. Serve with a green salad, if desired.

PREPARATION	COOKING	SERVINGS	FREEZES
20 MIN	1 H 15	6	–

\ | / ,

ALMOST TOO PRETTY FOR
A WEEKDAY MEAL!

/ / | \ `

ROASTED VEGETABLES

Oven-roasted vegetables are weeknight saviors! Work with vegetables that you already have on hand, making sure to cut them into uniform pieces and arranging them in a single layer on a non-stick sheet pan. Add a drizzle of vegetable oil and a pinch of salt and pepper, and pop them in the center of an oven preheated to 425°F (220°C). Stir the vegetables halfway through cooking. For extra browning, you can finish off cooking them under the broiler, keeping a close eye on them.

12 TO 15 MIN

30 TO 35 MIN

40 TO 45 MIN
↓

12 TO 15 MIN
↓

30 TO 35 MIN
↓

MINI TOFU-BEEF MEATLOAVES

SAUCE
2 tbsp (30 ml) ketchup or chili sauce
1 tbsp (15 ml) Dijon mustard
1 tbsp (15 ml) Worcestershire sauce

MEATLOAVES AND VEGETABLES
3 green onions, cut into pieces
3/4 lb (340 g) firm or extra-firm tofu, patted dry and cubed
3/4 lb (340 g) lean ground beef
1 egg
2 tbsp (30 ml) tomato paste
1 tbsp (15 ml) Dijon mustard
1 tbsp (15 ml) Worcestershire sauce
1 tsp celery salt
1 lb (450 g) green beans, trimmed
3/4 lb (340 g) baby potatoes, halved
1 tbsp (15 ml) vegetable oil

SAUCE
In a small bowl, combine all of the ingredients. Set aside.

MEATLOAVES AND VEGETABLES
With the rack in the middle position, preheat the oven to 400°F (200°C). Line a sheet pan with a silicone mat or parchment paper.

In a food processor, finely chop the green onions. Add the tofu and finely chop. Transfer to a large bowl.

Add the meat, egg, tomato paste, mustard, Worcestershire sauce and celery salt to the bowl. Season with pepper and mix until the mixture comes together. Divide the mixture into six equal parts and form into rectangles. Place the meatloaves on the sheet pan. Brush with the sauce.

In another large bowl, combine the green beans and potatoes with the oil. Season with salt and pepper. Arrange the vegetables around the meatloaves.

Bake for 30 to 35 minutes or until the meatloaves are cooked through.

PREPARATION	COOKING	SERVINGS	FREEZES
25 MIN	30 MIN	6	YES (MINI BEEF-TOFU MEATLOAVES)

A LOT CUTER MINI-SIZED.

CHEESESTEAK SUBS

1/2 lb	(225 g) white mushrooms, sliced
1	green bell pepper, seeded and cut into strips 1/4 inch (6 mm) thick
1	large onion, cut into strips 1/4 inch (6 mm) thick
2 tbsp	(30 ml) vegetable oil
2 tbsp	(30 ml) Worcestershire sauce
1 lb	(450 g) flap steak, cut into 2
4	submarine buns (each about 10 inches/25 cm long)
2 cups	(200 g) grated mozzarella cheese
	Flat-leaf parsley, finely chopped (optional)

With the rack in the middle position, preheat the oven to 425°F (220°C).

On a non-stick sheet pan, combine the mushrooms, bell pepper and onion with the oil and Worcestershire sauce. Season with salt and pepper. Bake for 10 minutes.

Stir the vegetables and move them away from the center of the sheet pan. Place the steaks in the center of the sheet pan. Season with salt and pepper. Bake for another 15 minutes or until the meat is cooked through and the vegetables are golden.

Remove from the oven and let sit for 10 minutes. Set the oven to broil.

On a work surface, cut the buns in half horizontally without going all the way through to the other side. Place on another sheet pan. Open the buns like a book and add the cheese. Broil for 3 minutes or until lightly browned. Thinly slice the steaks against the grain.

Top the subs with the meat and vegetables. Sprinkle with parsley, if desired.

PREPARATION	COOKING	SERVINGS	FREEZES
20 MIN	28 MIN	4	–

vegetable and
sausage poutine

WOW!
A GIANT POUTINE
TO SHARE.

VEGETABLE AND SAUSAGE POUTINE

SAUCE

2 tbsp	cornstarch
2 tbsp	(30 ml) water
3 tbsp	unsalted butter
2 tbsp	unbleached all-purpose flour
1	garlic clove, finely chopped
1 can	(10 oz/284 ml) concentrated beef broth
1 can	(10 oz/284 ml) concentrated chicken broth
1 pinch	cayenne pepper

POUTINE

2 1/2 lb	(1.1 kg) russet potatoes, peeled and cut into sticks 1/2 inch (1 cm) thick
1/2 lb	(225 g) white mushrooms, halved
1/4 cup	(60 ml) vegetable oil
2	zucchini, cut into thick spirals, then spirals cut into 5 shorter pieces
3	mild or spicy Italian sausages
3/4 lb	(340 g) cheese curds

SAUCE

In a small bowl, dissolve the cornstarch in the water.

In a pot over medium heat, melt the butter. Add the flour and cook for 3 minutes, stirring with a whisk, until the mixture (roux) is golden. Add the garlic and cook for another 30 seconds. Add both types of broth. Bring to a boil while stirring constantly. Add the cornstarch mixture and simmer for 3 minutes or until the sauce thickens. Add the cayenne pepper.

POUTINE

With both racks in the middle positions, preheat a convection oven to 450°F (230°C) (see note).

In a large bowl, toss the potatoes and mushrooms with 3 tbsp (45 ml) of the oil. Season with salt and pepper. Spread them out on two non-stick sheet pans without letting them overlap. Bake for 20 minutes.

Meanwhile, in a bowl, toss the zucchini with the remaining oil. Season with salt and pepper.

Gently stir the potatoes and mushrooms on the sheet pans. Add the sausages and rotate the sheet pans in the oven. Bake for 10 minutes. Flip the sausages and vegetables over. Bake for another 10 minutes or until the potatoes are golden and the sausages are cooked through. Cut the sausages into rounds. Set aside.

Transfer all of the potatoes and mushrooms onto one of the sheet pans. Add the zucchini and cheese. Mix well. Bake for another 5 minutes.

Add the sausage pieces to the sheet pan. Cover with the warm sauce.

NOTE *We opted for a convection oven for this recipe because you can cook more than one sheet pan at a time. In a traditional oven, switch the positions of the sheet pans throughout the cooking process. The cooking time may be slightly longer.*

PREPARATION	COOKING	SERVINGS	FREEZES
30 MIN	50 MIN	4 TO 6	–

PARMESAN-CRUSTED PORK CHOPS

VEGETABLES

3/4 lb	(340 g) baby potatoes, halved
1	acorn squash (about 1 1/4 lb/565 g), halved, seeded and cut into slices 1/2 inch (1 cm) thick
1	garlic clove, finely chopped
2 tbsp	(30 ml) vegetable oil

PARMESAN-CRUSTED PORK CHOPS

1 cup	(80 g) panko breadcrumbs
1/2 cup	(35 g) freshly grated Parmesan cheese
4	bone-in pork chops (each about 1 inch/2.5 cm thick)
1/4 cup	(60 ml) mayonnaise

CREAMY HONEY-MUSTARD SAUCE

1/4 cup	(60 ml) sour cream
2 tbsp	(30 ml) whole-grain mustard
2 tbsp	(30 ml) 35% cream
1 tbsp	(15 ml) honey

VEGETABLES

With both racks in the middle positions, preheat the oven to 425°F (220°C).

On a non-stick sheet pan, combine the potatoes and squash with the garlic and oil. Season with salt and pepper. Bake on the lower rack for 10 minutes. Flip the vegetables over.

PARMESAN-CRUSTED PORK CHOPS

Meanwhile, combine the breadcrumbs and cheese in a shallow bowl.

On a work surface, season the pork chops with salt and pepper. Brush both sides with the mayonnaise. Press each pork chop into the breadcrumb mixture and coat well. Place on a second non-stick sheet pan. Bake on the upper rack for 15 minutes. Continue roasting the vegetables at the same time for another 15 minutes.

Set the oven to broil. Cook for another 5 minutes or until the breadcrumbs are nicely browned.

CREAMY HONEY-MUSTARD SAUCE

In a bowl, whisk together all of the ingredients.

Serve the pork chops with the vegetables and sauce.

PREPARATION	COOKING	SERVINGS	FREEZES
20 MIN	30 MIN	4	–

GLAZED TOFU, EDAMAME AND VERMICELLI BOWL

MARINADE
2 tbsp	(30 ml)	tamari
2 tbsp	(30 ml)	balsamic vinegar
2 tbsp	(30 ml)	maple syrup
2 tbsp	(30 ml)	vegetable oil
1 tsp		garlic powder
1 lb	(450 g)	firm tofu, patted dry and diced (see note)

TOPPINGS
2		carrots, julienned
2		bell peppers, various colors, seeded and thinly sliced
1		onion, thinly sliced
1 tbsp	(15 ml)	vegetable oil
1 cup	(145 g)	shelled frozen edamame
5 oz	(140 g)	rice vermicelli
3 tbsp	(45 ml)	tamari
		Cilantro, finely chopped (optional)
		Sriracha (optional)

MARINADE

With the rack in the middle position, preheat the oven to 425°F (220°C).

In a large bowl, combine the tamari, vinegar, maple syrup, oil and garlic powder.

Add the tofu and mix well. Lay out on a non-stick sheet pan. Bake for 15 minutes or until the tofu is golden and the marinade has been absorbed, stirring halfway through.

TOPPINGS

In the same bowl, combine the carrots, bell peppers and onion with the oil. Arrange the vegetables around the glazed tofu on the sheet pan. Bake for another 10 minutes.

Meanwhile, in a pot of boiling water, add the edamame and vermicelli. Remove from the heat and let sit for 3 minutes or until tender. Drain well.

Add the edamame and vermicelli to the sheet pan. Drizzle with the tamari and mix well to combine the flavors. Adjust the seasoning. Serve in bowls. Sprinkle with cilantro and drizzle with Sriracha, if desired.

NOTE *The tofu can be replaced with two packages (8 1/2 oz/240 g each) frozen tempeh, thawed and diced. Or try 1 lb (450 g) diced boneless, skinless chicken breast. In this case, combine all of the marinade ingredients with the chicken and vegetables. Bake for 15 minutes, stirring halfway through. Do not add the extra tamari in the last step.*

PREPARATION	COOKING	SERVINGS	FREEZES
20 MIN	30 MIN	4 TO 6	–

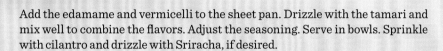

TOFU, TEMPEH, CHICKEN—THIS SHEET PAN WORKS WITH ALL.

HOISIN PORK TENDERLOIN

MEAT

1/3 cup	(75 ml) hoisin sauce
1/4 cup	(60 ml) vegetable oil
3 tbsp	(45 ml) reduced-sodium soy sauce
1 tsp	(5 ml) Sriracha
2	garlic cloves, finely chopped
2	pork tenderloins (each about 3/4 lb/340 g)

VEGETABLES

2	sweet potatoes, peeled and cut into 8 wedges each (about 1 1/4 lb/565 g total)
3/4 lb	(340 g) green beans, trimmed
2 tbsp	(30 ml) vegetable oil

MEAT

In a bowl, combine the hoisin, oil, soy sauce, Sriracha and garlic. Add the pork and mix well to coat in the marinade. Cover and let marinate for 8 hours or overnight in the refrigerator.

VEGETABLES

With the rack in the middle position, preheat the oven to 425°F (220°C).

In a large bowl, combine the sweet potatoes and green beans with the oil. Season with salt and pepper. Spread the vegetables out on a non-stick sheet pan. Bake for 10 minutes.

Flip the vegetables over and move them away from the center of the sheet pan. Place the pork in the center of the sheet pan and drizzle with the marinade. Bake for 15 minutes or until a thermometer inserted in the center of the pork reads 135°F (57°C). Remove from the heat, cover with foil and let sit for 5 minutes.

On a work surface, slice the pork and return to the sheet pan. Place the sheet pan at the center of the table and serve.

PREPARATION	MARINATING	COOKING	SERVINGS	FREEZES
20 MIN	8 H	25 MIN	4	–

EVERYTHING COOKS
TOGETHER.

PINEAPPLE CHICKEN

1/4 cup	(60 ml) maple syrup
1/4 cup	(60 ml) reduced-sodium soy sauce
1 tsp	(5 ml) sambal oelek
2 tbsp	finely chopped fresh ginger
2	garlic cloves, chopped
1 1/2 lb	(675 g) boneless, skinless chicken thighs, cubed (see note)
2	red bell peppers, seeded and cubed
1	head broccoli, cut into florets
1 tbsp	(15 ml) vegetable oil
2 cups	(290 g) cubed very ripe, fresh pineapple

In a bowl, combine the maple syrup, soy sauce, sambal oelek, ginger and garlic. Add the chicken and mix well to coat in the marinade. Cover and let marinate for 8 hours or overnight in the refrigerator.

With the rack in the middle position, preheat the oven to 425°F (220°C).

On a non-stick sheet pan, combine the bell peppers and broccoli with the oil. Season with salt and pepper. Spread out over one half of the sheet pan.

Drain the chicken from the marinade and set the marinade aside. Place the chicken and pineapple on the other half of the sheet pan.

Bake for 10 minutes. Flip the vegetables over. Brush the chicken with the reserved marinade and flip the pieces over. Bake for another 10 minutes or until the chicken is cooked through and browned.

Serve with white rice, if desired.

NOTE *Although chicken thighs are a more tender cut, you can replace them with the same quantity of boneless, skinless chicken breasts, cubed.*

PREPARATION	MARINATING	COOKING	SERVINGS	FREEZES
25 MIN	8 H	20 MIN	4	–

miso salmon with
sweet and sour
cashew-ginger topping

MISO SALMON
WITH SWEET AND SOUR
CASHEW-GINGER TOPPING

SWEET AND SOUR TOPPING

1	lime, washed
1	shallot, chopped
2	garlic cloves, chopped
1 tbsp	chopped fresh ginger
2 tbsp	(30 ml) vegetable oil
1/4 cup	(35 g) unsalted roasted cashews, finely chopped
2 tbsp	(30 ml) maple syrup
1/2 tsp	sambal oelek

MISO SALMON

1 1/2 lb	(675 g) salmon fillet with skin (about 3/4 inch/2 cm thick), cut into 4 pieces
1 tbsp	(15 ml) miso
1 tbsp	(15 ml) maple syrup
3/4 lb	(340 g) sugar snap peas, trimmed
1 tbsp	(15 ml) vegetable oil

With the rack in the middle position, preheat the oven to 425°F (220°C). Line a sheet pan with parchment paper or a silicone mat.

SWEET AND SOUR TOPPING

Finely grate the lime zest and place in a bowl. Using a knife, remove the pith and white membrane from the outside of the lime. Compost or discard the pith and membrane. Finely chop the lime flesh and add to the bowl of zest.

In a small pot over medium-high heat, brown the shallot, garlic and ginger in the oil while stirring with a wooden spoon. Add the cashews and maple syrup. Cook for another minute. Pour into the bowl of lime zest and flesh. Add the sambal oelek. Season with salt. Set aside at room temperature.

MISO SALMON

Place the salmon pieces on the sheet pan. In a bowl, combine the miso and maple syrup. Using a pastry brush, cover the fish with the miso mixture. Bake for 4 minutes.

In a bowl, toss the sugar snap peas with the oil. Season with salt and pepper. Arrange the peas around the salmon and bake for another 4 minutes or until the fish is cooked to the desired doneness.

Serve with the sweet and sour topping and basmati rice, if desired.

PREPARATION	COOKING	SERVINGS	FREEZES
15 MIN	15 MIN	4	–

COUSCOUS WITH VEGETABLES AND CHICKPEAS

2	carrots, diced
2	stalks celery, diced
1	onion, finely chopped
1/4 cup	(30 g) sliced almonds
2 tbsp	(30 ml) vegetable oil
1 tsp	ras-el-hanout (see note)
1 can	(19 oz/540 ml) chickpeas, rinsed and drained
1 1/2 cups	(375 ml) chicken broth
2 tbsp	butter
2 tbsp	currants
1 1/2 cups	(300 g) toasted couscous (recipe p. 24)
1/4 cup	(10 g) finely chopped parsley

With the rack in the middle position, preheat a convection oven to 425°F (220°C) (see note). Line a sheet pan with a parchment paper or silicone mat.

In a bowl, combine the carrots, celery, onion, almonds, oil and ras-el-hanout. Season with salt and pepper. Spread the mixture out on the sheet pan. Bake for 20 minutes, stirring twice during cooking. Add the chickpeas and mix well. Bake for another 5 minutes or until the vegetables are golden and the chickpeas are heated through.

Meanwhile, in a pot, bring the broth, butter and currants to a boil. Remove from the heat and add the couscous. Cover and let sit for 5 minutes. Fluff the couscous grains with a fork. Season with salt and pepper.

In a large serving bowl, combine the couscous, vegetable and chickpea mixture and parsley. Adjust the seasoning. Serve with grilled merguez sausages, if desired.

NOTES *Ras-el-hanout is a spice blend that contains a mix of coriander, allspice, cumin, black pepper, cardamom, cinnamon, turmeric, nutmeg, ginger, cloves and cayenne pepper. The mix of spices will vary from one brand to another.*

The vegetables and chickpeas will bake more evenly when cooked on convection. For a traditional oven, toss often during cooking.

PREPARATION	COOKING	SERVINGS	FREEZES
15 MIN	25 MIN	4	–

CHICKEN "TAJINE"

3/4 lb	(340 g) boneless, skinless chicken thighs, cubed (see note)
3/4 lb	(340 g) merguez sausages
2	onions, cut into thin wedges
2	garlic cloves, chopped
1 tsp	curry powder
1/4 tsp	fennel seeds, crushed
3 tbsp	(45 ml) olive oil
2	zucchini, cut into thin ribbons on a mandoline
1/4 cup	(50 g) diced dried apricots
1/4 cup	(10 g) cilantro leaves
1	lemon, cut into wedges, for serving

With the rack in the middle position, preheat the oven to 425°F (220°C). Line a sheet pan with parchment paper or a silicone mat.

On the sheet pan, combine the chicken, sausages, onions and garlic with the curry powder, crushed fennel and 2 tbsp (30 ml) of the oil. Bake for 25 minutes, stirring halfway through.

In a bowl, combine the zucchini and apricots with the remaining oil. Add the zucchini mixture to the sheet pan. Bake for another 5 minutes or until the chicken is cooked through and the zucchini is tender. Season with salt and pepper.

Top with the cilantro and serve with the lemon wedges.

NOTE *Chicken thighs work best for this recipe. They will be juicier and more tender than chicken breast.*

PREPARATION	COOKING	SERVINGS	FREEZES
20 MIN	30 MIN	4	–

IN TURKISH, SHAWARMA MEANS
"TURNING." ON THE SHEET PAN,
IT TURNS ONLY ONCE!

SHAWARMA-STYLE TOFU WITH MEDITERRANEAN SALAD

TOFU SHAWARMA

1/4 cup	(60 ml) olive oil
1 tbsp	(15 ml) honey
2 tbsp	curry powder
1 1/2 tsp	ground cinnamon
1/2 tsp	ground allspice
2	blocks (3/4 lb/340 g each) extra-firm tofu, thinly sliced
2	onions, thinly sliced
2	garlic cloves, chopped
2 tbsp	(30 ml) lemon juice

MEDITERRANEAN SALAD

2 cups	(280 g) cherry tomatoes, halved
2	green onions, finely chopped
1	yellow bell pepper, seeded and diced
1/2	English cucumber, diced
1/2 cup	(25 g) finely chopped cilantro
2 tbsp	(30 ml) olive oil
2 tbsp	(30 ml) lemon juice
1/2 tsp	ground sumac

TOFU SHAWARMA

With the rack in the middle position, preheat a convection oven to 450°F (230°C) (see note). Line a sheet pan with foil (see note p. 10).

In a large bowl, combine the oil, honey and spices. Add the tofu, onions and garlic. Mix to coat well. The tofu will fall apart into irregular pieces. Season with salt and pepper. Spread the mixture out on the sheet pan. Bake for 20 to 25 minutes, stirring halfway through. Drizzle with the lemon juice.

MEDITERRANEAN SALAD

Meanwhile, in a bowl, combine all of the ingredients. Season with salt and pepper.

Serve the tofu with the salad, hummus and flatbread sprinkled with sumac, if desired.

NOTE *The tofu will bake more evenly when cooked on convection. For a traditional oven, toss often during cooking.*

PREPARATION	COOKING	SERVINGS	FREEZES
20 MIN	20 TO 25 MIN	4	—

cauliflower tacos

shrimp tacos

TWO KINDS OF TACOS:
VEGGIE AND SHRIMP!

CAULIFLOWER TACOS

CAULIFLOWER
1	large cauliflower (about 2.2 lb/1 kg), cut into very small florets
1	bunch radishes (about 7 oz/200 g), halved or quartered
1	red onion, cut into thin wedges
2 tbsp	(30 ml) vegetable oil
1 tsp	coriander seeds, crushed
1 tsp	cumin seeds, crushed
1/2 tsp	ground turmeric
1 can	(19 oz/540 ml) black beans, rinsed and drained

CILANTRO CREMA
1 cup	(250 ml) plain Greek yogurt
2 tbsp	(30 ml) lime juice
1/2 cup	(25 g) finely chopped cilantro
1	small garlic clove, finely chopped

TACOS
8	soft flour tortillas (each about 6 inches/15 cm in diameter), warmed
1	avocado, diced and lightly tossed with lemon juice
1	tomato, diced
1/4 cup	(40 g) roasted pumpkin seeds
1	lime, cut into wedges
	Tabasco-style jalapeño sauce, to taste

CAULIFLOWER

With the rack in the middle position, preheat the oven to 425°F (220°C). Line a sheet pan with foil (see note p. 10).

On the sheet pan, combine the vegetables with the oil and spices. Season generously with salt and pepper.

Bake for 18 minutes or until the vegetables are golden, stirring halfway through. Add the black beans and bake for another 2 minutes to heat them through.

CILANTRO CREMA

Meanwhile, in a bowl, combine all of the ingredients. Season with salt and pepper.

ASSEMBLY

Place the vegetable mixture, tortillas, avocado, tomato, pumpkin seeds, lime wedges, jalapeño sauce and cilantro crema in the center of the table. Let everyone build their own tacos.

PREPARATION	COOKING	SERVINGS	FREEZES
30 MIN	20 MIN	4	–

SHRIMP TACOS

TACOS

3 cups	(255 g) thinly sliced green cabbage
2 tbsp	(30 ml) lemon juice
1/4 tsp	salt
1 1/2 lb	(675 g) medium shrimp (20–40), shelled and deveined
1 tbsp	chili powder
1 1/2 cups	(225 g) frozen corn kernels
4	green onions, thinly sliced, whites and greens separated
1	lemon, cut into wedges
1	small jalapeño pepper, thinly sliced
2 tbsp	(30 ml) vegetable oil
8	soft corn tortillas (each about 6 inches/15 cm in diameter), warmed

AVOCADO CREAM

2	ripe avocados
1/2 cup	(125 ml) sour cream
1/2 cup	(25 g) finely chopped cilantro

TACOS

With the rack in the middle position, preheat the oven to 425°F (220°C).

In a bowl, combine the cabbage with the lemon juice and salt. Let marinate until ready to serve.

In another bowl, combine the shrimp and chili powder. Season with salt.

Spread the shrimp out on a non-stick sheet pan. Add the corn, whites of the green onions, lemon wedges and jalapeño. Drizzle with the oil. Bake for 10 minutes.

AVOCADO CREAM

Meanwhile, in a blender, purée the avocados with the sour cream and cilantro until smooth. Season with salt and pepper. Add half of the avocado cream to the bowl of cabbage and mix well.

ASSEMBLY

Spread the remaining avocado cream over the tortillas. Top with the shrimp mixture, cabbage salad and remaining green onions. Drizzle with the juice of the warm lemon wedges.

PREPARATION	COOKING	SERVINGS	FREEZES
30 MIN	10 MIN	4	–

MY GIRLS DIDN'T SUSPECT A THING: THESE ARE JUST AS GOOD AS ON THE STOVETOP, MINUS THE MESS!

white meat

dark meat

CHICKEN FAJITAS

CHICKEN

1	large red onion, cut into very thin wedges
2	bell peppers, various colors, seeded and cut into strips
2 tbsp	(30 ml) vegetable oil
1 1/2 lb	(675 g) mix of boneless, skinless chicken thighs and breasts, cut into strips (see note)
1 tbsp	chili powder

TOPPINGS

8	medium soft tortillas (each about 8 inches/20 cm in diameter)
1	lime, cut into wedges
1/4 cup	(10 g) cilantro leaves
2 cups	(200 g) grated mild orange cheddar cheese
	Homemade or store-bought salsa, to taste
	Homemade or store-bought guacamole, to taste
	Sour cream, to taste

CHICKEN

With the rack in the middle position, preheat the oven to 425°F (220°C).

On a non-stick sheet pan, combine the onion and bell peppers with 1 tbsp (15 ml) of the oil.

In a bowl, combine the chicken, chili powder and remaining oil. Add to the sheet pan with the vegetables. Season with salt and pepper. Bake for 20 minutes or until the chicken is cooked, stirring halfway through.

TOPPINGS

Meanwhile, wrap the tortillas in foil. Place directly on the oven rack for the last 5 minutes of the chicken cooking time.

Remove the sheet pan from the oven and add the lime wedges and cilantro to the pan. Place in the center of the table along with the tortillas, cheese, salsa, guacamole and sour cream. Let everyone build their own fajitas.

NOTE *Cut the chicken breasts in half horizontally before cutting into strips.*

PREPARATION	COOKING	SERVINGS	FREEZES
25 MIN	20 MIN	4	—

giant breakfast sandwiches

crispy hash brown (rösti)

SHEET PAN
BRUNCH

Having the time to quietly drink a coffee while brunch is in the oven—that's what morning cooking with the sheet pan is all about!

CRISPY HASH BROWN (RÖSTI)

1/4 cup	(55 g) butter, melted
3 lb	(1.4 kg) potatoes, peeled (about 6 large potatoes)
1	egg
1 cup	(100 g) grated Gruyère cheese

With the rack in the middle position, preheat the oven to 425°F (220°C). Line a sheet pan with parchment paper and brush with half of the butter (2 tbsp).

Using a spiralizer, cut the potatoes into thin spirals. In a large bowl, combine the potatoes and remaining butter with the egg and cheese. Season with salt and pepper. Spread the mixture out on the sheet pan.

Bake for 35 minutes or until the potatoes are nicely browned.

PREPARATION	COOKING	SERVINGS	FREEZES
20 MIN	35 MIN	6 TO 8	–

THEY'RE EVEN CRISPIER COOKED ON A SHEET PAN.

CHEDDAR, BACON AND BAGUETTE STRATA

1	baguette
6	eggs
1/4 cup	(60 ml) milk
1/4 cup	(60 ml) 35% cream
1/2 cup	(50 g) grated cheddar cheese
1/2 cup	(50 g) cooked bacon, cut into small dice (recipe p. 26)
2 tbsp	finely chopped chives

With the rack in the middle position, preheat the oven to 375°F (190°C).

On a work surface, cut the top off the baguette. Remove about 2 cups (60 g) of the crumb from the inside of the bread, leaving a 1/2-inch (1 cm) border of crumb all around the crust. Place the baguette on a non-stick sheet pan. Save the crumb for another use.

In a bowl, whisk together the eggs, milk and cream with the cheese. Add the bacon and chives. Season with salt and pepper. Pour the mixture into the hollowed-out bread. Let soak for 5 minutes. If you have any remaining mixture in the bowl, pour it into the bread.

Bake for 15 to 20 minutes or until the egg mixture is cooked. Let sit for 10 minutes. Cut into pieces and serve.

PREPARATION	COOKING	SERVINGS	FREEZES
20 MIN	15 MIN	4 TO 6	–

ALL-DRESSED
BREAKFAST BAKE

6 slices	bacon, thinly sliced crosswise
1	sweet potato, peeled and diced
1	onion, thinly sliced
1	red bell pepper, seeded and cubed
5	plum tomatoes, diced
3 tbsp	(45 ml) tomato paste
2 tbsp	(30 ml) molasses
1 tsp	(5 ml) harissa
1 can	(19 oz/540 ml) white beans, rinsed and drained
6	eggs
1/4 cup	(10 g) finely chopped flat-leaf parsley

With the rack in the middle position, preheat the oven to 400°F (200°C).

On a non-stick sheet pan, combine the bacon, sweet potato, onion and bell pepper. Season with salt and pepper. Bake for 30 minutes, stirring halfway through.

Meanwhile, in a bowl, combine the tomatoes, tomato paste, molasses and harissa. Add to the sheet pan and toss well to coat the vegetables. Bake for another 15 minutes.

Remove from the oven. Add the white beans and stir gently. Using the back of a spoon, make six wells in the vegetable mixture. Break an egg into each well. Season the eggs with salt and pepper. Bake for another 6 to 7 minutes or until the eggs are cooked.

Sprinkle with the parsley. Serve with toast, if desired.

PREPARATION	COOKING	SERVINGS	FREEZES
20 MIN	55 MIN	6	–

CRISPY HAM
AND CHEESE WRAP

2 tbsp	(30 ml) vegetable oil
10	large tortillas (9 inches/23 cm in diameter)
3 tbsp	(45 ml) whole-grain mustard
5 cups	(500 g) grated Swiss cheese
1 lb	(450 g) white ham, thinly sliced
1 cup	(250 ml) caramelized onions (recipe p. 21)

With the rack in the middle position, preheat the oven to 400°F (200°C).

Brush a non-stick sheet pan with half of the oil (1 tbsp/15 ml). Cover the surface of the sheet pan with eight tortillas, letting them overlap slightly (six of the tortillas should be hanging halfway off the sheet pan). Brush the surface of the tortillas on the sheet pan with the mustard. Top with half of the cheese (2 1/2 cups/250 g). Cover with the ham and onions. Sprinkle with the remaining cheese. Place the remaining tortillas in the center. Fold over the overhanging tortillas to completely cover the filling.

Brush the top of the sandwich with the remaining oil. Place a second sheet pan over top. Weigh down the second sheet pan with a cast-iron skillet (or another heavy, ovenproof object).

Bake for 30 minutes. Remove the cast-iron skillet and top sheet pan. Bake the sandwich for another 5 minutes or until nicely golden. Let cool for 5 minutes. Cut into pieces and serve.

PREPARATION	COOKING	SERVINGS	FREEZES
20 MIN	35 MIN	8	–

IT'S LIKE A GIANT PANINI FOR EIGHT!

ASPARAGUS QUICHE

1 1/2 cups	(225 g) unbleached all-purpose flour
1/4 tsp	salt
1/2 cup	(115 g) cold unsalted butter, diced
1/2 cup	(125 ml) plain yogurt
1/4 cup	(60 ml) ice water
8	eggs
1 cup	(250 ml) 35% or 15% cream
3/4 lb	(340 g) small asparagus, trimmed and blanched

In a food processor, combine the flour and salt. Add the butter and pulse a few times until it forms pea-sized pieces. Add the yogurt and water. Pulse just until the dough starts coming together. Add more water as needed. Remove the dough from the food processor and form into a rectangle.

On a floured work surface, roll the dough into a 15 × 12-inch (38 × 30 cm) rectangle. Line a small 13 × 9-inch (33 × 23 cm) sheet pan with the dough. Refrigerate for 30 minutes.

With the rack in the lowest position, preheat the oven to 400°F (200°C).

Prick the dough all over with a fork. Cover the dough with a piece of foil and fill with dried peas or pie weights.

Bake for 20 minutes. Remove the peas and foil. Bake for another 5 minutes or until the crust is golden. Set aside.

In a bowl, whisk together the eggs and cream. Season with salt and pepper. Pour the egg mixture into the crust. Top with the asparagus.

Bake for 20 to 25 minutes or until the filling is cooked and the crust is golden. Let rest for 5 minutes before unmolding.

Cut into long rectangles. Serve as is or with smoked salmon, crème fraîche and dill or with white ham, mustard and chopped chives, if desired.

PREPARATION	CHILLING	COOKING	SERVINGS	FREEZES
30 MIN	30 MIN	45 MIN	6	–

BETTER THAN A PIE DISH, A SHEET PAN
LETS YOU USE WHOLE ASPARAGUS.
PRETTY... AND DELICIOUS!

GIANT BREAKFAST SANDWICHES

DIJONNAISE

1/2 cup	(125 ml) mayonnaise	
1 tbsp	(15 ml) Dijon mustard	

PATTIES

1 1/2 lb	(675 g) medium-lean ground pork	
3	slices white or whole wheat bread, finely chopped	
8	eggs	
1 tbsp	(15 ml) Dijon mustard	
1 tbsp	(15 ml) maple syrup	
1/2 tsp	salt	

TOPPINGS

6	English muffins, halved horizontally
6	leaves lettuce
6	slices tomato
6	slices cooked bacon, warmed (recipe p. 26)

DIJONNAISE

In a small bowl, combine the mayonnaise and mustard. Refrigerate until ready to serve.

PATTIES

With both racks in the middle positions, preheat a convection oven to 425°F (220°C) (see note).

In a large bowl, using your hands, combine the ground pork with the bread, two eggs, mustard, maple syrup and salt. Season generously with pepper.

On a work surface, form the meat mixture into six patties about 4 1/2 inches (11.5 cm) in diameter (see note) and place on a sheet pan lined with a silicone mat. Using the bottom of a glass or a small ramekin 3 inches (7.5 cm) in diameter, make a well at the center of each patty about 1/2 inch (1 cm) deep.

Bake on the lower rack of the oven for 12 minutes. Remove the sheet pan from the oven and crack an egg into each well. Season the eggs with salt and pepper. Bake for another 10 to 12 minutes or until the egg whites are set.

TOPPINGS

Meanwhile, place the English muffins on a second sheet pan, cut-side up. Bake on the upper rack of the oven for 5 minutes or until lightly toasted.

Spread the insides of the English muffins with the Dijonnaise. Layer on the lettuce, tomato, bacon and patties. Close the sandwiches. Cut in half and serve immediately.

NOTES *We opted for a convection oven for this recipe because you can cook more than one baking sheet at a time. In a traditional oven, the cooking time may be slightly longer.*

A burger press is ideal for forming patties with a well in the center.

PREPARATION	COOKING	MAKES	FREEZES
35 MIN	22 MIN	6 SANDWICHES	–

YOU WON'T HAVE TO GET OUT TWO FRYING PANS AND THE TOASTER TO MAKE THESE!

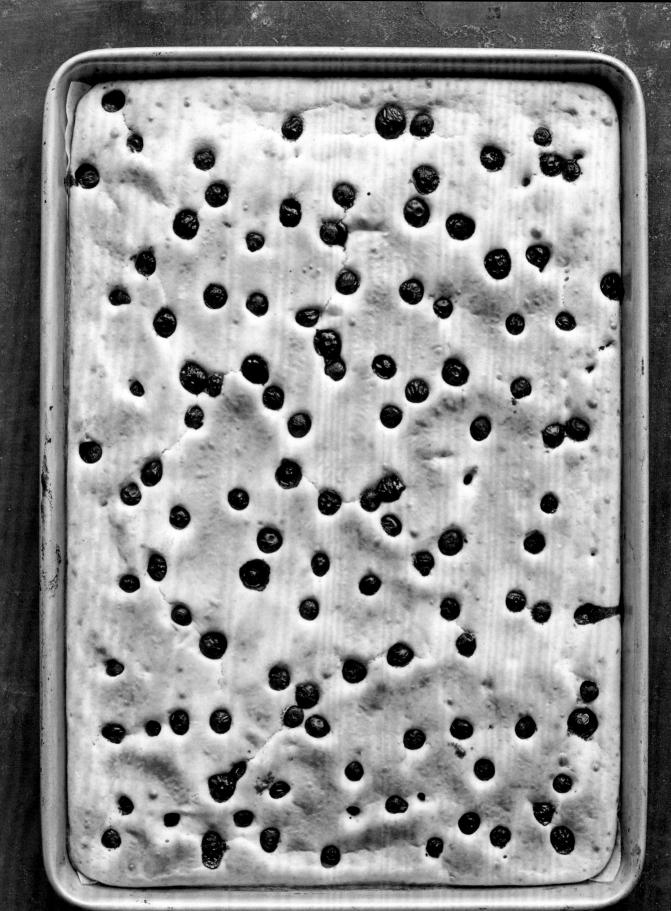

BLUEBERRY PANCAKE

1/4 cup	(55 g) butter, melted
2 1/2 cups	(375 g) unbleached all-purpose flour
1 tsp	baking powder
1 tsp	baking soda
3	eggs
1/2 cup	(65 g) icing sugar
2 1/4 cups	(560 ml) buttermilk (see note)
2 cups	(300 g) fresh blueberries

With the rack in the middle position, preheat a convection oven to 450°F (230°C) (see note). Line a sheet pan with parchment paper and brush with half of the butter (2 tbsp).

In a bowl, combine the flour, baking powder and baking soda.

In another bowl, beat the eggs and icing sugar with an electric mixer for 5 minutes. With the machine running on low speed, add the remaining butter. Add half of the buttermilk, then the dry ingredients. Add the remaining buttermilk and mix until the batter is smooth. Using a spatula, fold in half of the blueberries. Spread the batter out on the sheet pan. Sprinkle with the remaining blueberries.

Bake for 12 minutes or until the pancake is slightly golden.

Delicious served with maple syrup.

NOTES *If you do not have buttermilk, add 2 tbsp (30 ml) white vinegar or lemon juice to 2 1/4 cups (560 ml) milk. Let sit for 5 minutes. Stir and use.*

You can omit the blueberries to enjoy a plain pancake.

We prefer using a convection oven for this recipe to get a perfectly golden pancake. Baking in a conventional oven will result in a paler, but just as delicious, pancake for the same amount of baking time.

Leftover slices of pancake can be reheated in the toaster the next day.

PREPARATION	COOKING	SERVINGS	FREEZES
15 MIN	12 MIN	6 TO 8	YES

~~~

PERFECT WHEN HOSTING A CROWD FOR BREAKFAST.

~~~

PREP THE NIGHT
BEFORE, THEN BAKE
FOR 30 MINUTES
IN THE MORNING.

cinnamon buns

CINNAMON BUNS

DOUGH

1 1/2 cups	(375 ml) milk
2 tsp	instant yeast
1	egg
1 tsp	(5 ml) vanilla
3 cups	(450 g) unbleached all-purpose flour
1/4 cup	(55 g) sugar
1/2 tsp	salt
6 tbsp	(85 g) unsalted butter, softened

FILLING

1 cup	(210 g) brown sugar
2 tsp	ground cinnamon
6 tbsp	(85 g) unsalted butter, softened

ICING

1 cup	(130 g) icing sugar
1 tbsp	(15 ml) milk

DOUGH

In a small bowl, combine the milk and yeast (see note). Let sit for 5 minutes to rehydrate and dissolve the yeast. Add the egg and vanilla. Mix well.

In a large bowl, using a wooden spoon, or in a stand mixer fitted with the dough hook, combine the flour, sugar and salt. Add the milk mixture and mix until the dough starts coming together.

Gradually add the butter and on a lightly floured work surface, or in the stand mixer with the dough hook, knead the dough for 5 minutes. The dough will be soft and slightly sticky. Put the dough back in the bowl (see note).

Cover the bowl with plastic wrap. Let rise for 30 minutes at room temperature. Refrigerate for 8 hours or overnight.

FILLING

In a bowl, combine the brown sugar and cinnamon.

On a floured work surface, roll the dough out to a 13-inch (33 cm) square about 1/2 inch (1 cm) thick.

Spread the butter over the dough and top with the brown sugar mixture. Roll the dough into a cylinder. Cut into 12 slices.

Place the slices, flat-side down, on a small, generously buttered 13 × 9-inch (33 × 23 cm) sheet pan. Let rise for 30 minutes at room temperature or until doubled in volume.

With the rack in the middle position, preheat the oven to 350°F (180°C).

Bake the cinnamon buns for 30 minutes or until golden. Let cool on a wire rack.

ICING

In a bowl, combine the icing sugar and milk until smooth. Add more milk as needed. When ready to serve, spread the icing over the buns. Best eaten the day of, the buns can, however, keep for 2 days in an airtight container at room temperature.

NOTES *The instant yeast is dissolved in the milk before combining it with the rest of the ingredients because the butter in the dough will otherwise prevent the yeast from fully dissolving.*

If desired, add 1/4 cup (35 g) raisins or 1/4 cup (40 g) dried cranberries to the dough after kneading it.

PREPARATION	RISING	CHILLING	COOKING	MAKES	FREEZES
40 MIN	1 H	8 H	30 MIN	12 BUNS	–

cinnamon-raisin
scones

baked apple butter

CINNAMON-RAISIN SCONES

2 cups	(300 g) unbleached all-purpose flour
1/4 cup	(55 g) brown sugar
1/3 cup	(45 g) currants or raisins
1 tsp	baking powder
1/2 tsp	baking soda
1/4 tsp	salt
1/4 tsp	ground cinnamon
1/2 cup	(115 g) cold unsalted butter, diced
3/4 cup	(180 ml) buttermilk, plus more for brushing
1/2 tsp	vanilla
1 tbsp	sugar, for sprinkling

With the rack in the middle position, preheat the oven to 400°F (200°C). Line a sheet pan with parchment paper.

In a food processor or in a bowl, combine the dry ingredients. Add the butter and mix until it forms pea-sized pieces. Add the buttermilk and vanilla. Mix just until the flour is moistened. Do not overmix the dough.

On the sheet pan, spread the dough with your fingers, or a rolling pin, into an 8-inch (20 cm) circle about 1 inch (2.5 cm) thick. Using a knife, cut the dough into eight triangles. Using a pastry brush, cover the scones with buttermilk and sprinkle with the sugar.

Bake for 18 to 20 minutes or until the scones are golden. Let cool on a wire rack. Serve with baked apple butter (recipe opposite), if desired. The scones are best enjoyed the day they are made but will keep for 2 days in an airtight container at room temperature.

PREPARATION	COOKING	MAKES	FREEZES
20 MIN	18 MIN	8 SCONES	YES

BAKED APPLE BUTTER

4 1/2 lb (2 kg) Cortland apples, unpeeled, seeded and cubed
2 tbsp sugar, or more to taste

With the rack in the middle position, preheat the oven to 350°F (180°C). Line a sheet pan with a silicone mat (see note).

Spread the apple cubes out on the sheet pan. Bake for 1 hour or until tender, stirring twice during cooking.

In a food processor, purée the hot apples with the sugar for 5 minutes until smooth. Use a spatula to scrape down the sides of the food processor as needed. Strain through a sieve, if desired. Transfer to airtight containers. The apple butter will keep for 1 month in the refrigerator. Spread over toast, crêpes or cinnamon-raisin scones (recipe opposite).

NOTE *We prefer using a silicone mat rather than parchment paper to encourage moisture evaporation during cooking.*

PREPARATION	COOKING	MAKES	FREEZES
25 MIN	1 H	4 CUPS (1 L), APPROX.	YES

FRENCH TOAST

1/4 cup	(55 g) unsalted butter, melted
4	eggs
1/4 cup	(55 g) brown sugar
1 1/2 cups	(375 ml) milk
1/2 tsp	vanilla
6	large slices day-old crusty bread (about 3/4 inch/2 cm thick)

With the rack in the middle position, preheat the oven to 425°F (220°C). Line a sheet pan with a silicone mat or parchment paper and brush with the butter.

In a large bowl, whisk together the eggs, brown sugar, milk and vanilla until smooth.

Dip the bread slices in the mixture one at a time, letting each one soak for 2 minutes or until completely saturated. Lay the bread out on the sheet pan (see note).

Bake for 15 minutes or until the bottoms are golden. Flip the slices over. Bake for another 10 to 15 minutes or until nicely browned on both sides.

Delicious served with maple syrup or a fruit coulis.

NOTE *If preparing the French toast in advance, you can cover the sheet pan at this point and refrigerate overnight.*

PREPARATION	COOKING	SERVINGS	FREEZES
20 MIN	25 MIN	6	–

~~~

NO MORE STANDING OVER THE STOVE, FLIPPING ALL THOSE PIECES OF TOAST.

~~~

roasted Brussels sprouts

rack of pork loin with roasted shallot dressing

SHEET PAN
ENTERTAINING

Perfect for serving family-style, we love placing the sheet pan in the center of the table!

ROASTED SQUASH
WITH RICOTTA

1	large butternut squash (about 3 1/2 lb/1.6 kg), halved and seeded
2 cups	(100 g) baguette torn into small pieces
2 tbsp	(30 ml) olive oil
2 tbsp	roasted almonds
2 tbsp	pumpkin seeds
1/2 tsp	ground fennel seeds
1/2	bulb fennel, thinly sliced
1	small shallot, thinly sliced
2 tsp	(10 ml) white wine vinegar
1 cup	(260 g) ricotta cheese
	Fennel fronds (optional)

With the rack in the middle position, preheat the oven to 425°F (220°C). Line a sheet pan with parchment paper or a silicone mat.

Season the squash halves with salt and pepper. Place cut-side down on the sheet pan. Bake for 45 minutes or until fork-tender. Remove the parchment paper and flip the squash over.

In a bowl, combine the bread, oil, almonds, pumpkin seeds and ground fennel seeds. Season with salt and pepper. Arrange around the squash on the sheet pan. Bake for 8 minutes or until the bread is crispy.

In another bowl, combine the sliced fennel, shallot and vinegar. Season with salt and pepper.

Divide the ricotta between the squash halves. Top with the bread mixture and fennel salad. Sprinkle with fennel fronds, if desired. Cut into slices and serve immediately.

PREPARATION	COOKING	SERVINGS	FREEZES
25 MIN	55 MIN	6 TO 8 APPETIZERS OR SIDE DISHES	–

SHEET PAN,
MEET SQUASH, YOUR
NEW BEST FRIEND.

HOW ABOUT SAVING
AN HOUR BY COOKING BEETS
ON THE SHEET PAN?

BEET, CHICKPEA AND POMEGRANATE SALAD

3	large beets, peeled and thinly sliced on a mandoline
3 tbsp	(45 ml) olive oil
1 can	(19 oz/540 ml) chickpeas, rinsed and drained
1	shallot, thinly sliced
2 tsp	curry powder
2 cups	(50 g) arugula
1 tbsp	(15 ml) pomegranate molasses or balsamic vinegar
1/4 cup	(45 g) pomegranate seeds

With the rack in the middle position, preheat the oven to 400°F (200°C). Line a sheet pan with foil (see note p. 10).

On the sheet pan, toss the beets with 2 tbsp (30 ml) of the oil. Season with salt and pepper. Bake for 20 minutes, stirring halfway through.

Meanwhile, in a bowl, combine the chickpeas, shallot, curry powder and remaining oil. Season with salt and pepper. Add to the sheet pan and bake for another 5 minutes. Let cool.

Top the cooled beets with the arugula. Drizzle with the pomegranate molasses and sprinkle with the pomegranate seeds.

NOTE *This vegan, gluten-free salad is the perfect appetizer to serve your dinner guests. It's also great as a light lunch.*

PREPARATION	COOKING	SERVINGS	FREEZES
20 MIN	25 MIN	4	–

barley with root vegetables
and grilled halloumi

BARLEY WITH ROOT VEGETABLES AND GRILLED HALLOUMI

BARLEY

1 cup	(200 g) hulled barley, rinsed and drained
1 tbsp	(15 ml) olive oil
2 cups	(500 ml) vegetable broth or water
1	bay leaf

ROOT VEGETABLES AND HALLOUMI

8	small cipollini onions, peeled and kept whole
1	small acorn squash with skin, seeded and cut into wedges 1/2 inch (1 cm) thick (see note)
4	yellow beets, peeled and cut into slices 1/4 inch (5 mm) thick
4	parsnips, peeled and cut lengthwise into slices 1/4 inch (5 mm) thick
3 tbsp	(45 ml) olive oil
4	sprigs thyme
3/4 lb	(340 g) halloumi cheese, at room temperature, cut into 4 large rectangles 1/2 inch (1 cm) thick and patted dry
2 cups	(90 g) Brussels sprout leaves, blanched

DRESSING

1/4 cup	(60 ml) mayonnaise
2 tbsp	(30 ml) maple syrup
2 tbsp	(30 ml) apple cider vinegar
2 tbsp	(30 ml) tahini

With both racks in the middle positions, preheat the oven to 425°F (220°C).

BARLEY

In a small pot over medium-high heat, cook the barley in the oil for 1 minute while stirring. Add the broth and bay leaf. Bring to a boil. Simmer, uncovered, over medium-low heat for 30 minutes or until the liquid is absorbed and the barley is al dente. Fluff the grains of barley with a fork.

ROOT VEGETABLES AND HALLOUMI

Meanwhile, on a non-stick sheet pan, toss the onions, the squash, the beets and the parsnips with 2 tbsp (30 ml) of the oil. Season with salt and pepper. Add the thyme. Bake on the upper rack for 10 minutes. Remove from the oven. Flip the vegetables over.

Place the halloumi slices directly on another sheet pan (with no silicone mat or parchment paper). Brush with the remaining oil. Bake the halloumi on the lower rack and the vegetables on the upper rack for 5 minutes. Flip the halloumi over and bake for another 5 minutes or until nicely golden. It is possible that the vegetables will be cooked at this point. If so, remove from the oven. If not, continue to cook them.

Add the barley to the vegetables sheet pan and mix gently.

DRESSING

In a small bowl, whisk together all of the ingredients. Season with salt and pepper.

Add the halloumi and Brussels sprout leaves to the sheet pan of barley and vegetables. Serve with the dressing.

NOTES *The acorn squash can be replaced with two delicata squash.*

The barley and vegetables can be served at room temperature, but the halloumi is best served hot.

PREPARATION	COOKING	SERVINGS	FREEZES
35 MIN	30 MIN	4	–

LAYERED GARLIC CREAM POTATOES, KALE AND FISH

GARLIC CREAM

1 cup	(250 ml) chicken broth
3/4 cup	(180 ml) 35% cream
4	garlic cloves, chopped
2	sprigs thyme, plus more for serving
2	bay leaves
1/4 tsp	ground nutmeg

LAYERED POTATOES, KALE AND FISH

2 lb	(900 g) yellow-fleshed potatoes, peeled or unpeeled, cut on a mandoline into slices 1/8 inch (3 mm)
2 1/2 cups	(75 g) thinly sliced kale leaves, stems removed
1 tbsp	(15 ml) olive oil
1 1/2 lb	(675 g) haddock fillets (or other white fish), cut into 4 to 6 pieces, as needed

With the rack in the middle position, preheat the oven to 425°F (220°C). Butter a small 13 × 9-inch (33 × 23 cm) non-stick sheet pan.

GARLIC CREAM

In a pot, bring all the ingredients to a boil. Simmer for 2 minutes. Cover and remove from the heat.

LAYERED POTATOES, KALE AND FISH

Cover the sheet pan with slices of potato. Season with salt and pepper. Repeat with two more layers of potatoes, seasoning each layer with salt and pepper.

Pour the hot cream mixture over the potatoes. Cover with foil. Bake for 45 to 50 minutes or until the potatoes are cooked.

In a bowl, toss the kale with the oil. Season with salt and pepper.

Remove the foil from the potatoes, as well as the bay leaves and thyme. Spread the kale over the potatoes and top with the fish. Season with salt and pepper.

Bake for 10 minutes or until the fish is cooked through. Let sit for 10 minutes before serving. Garnish with thyme, if desired.

PREPARATION	COOKING	SERVINGS	FREEZES
30 MIN	1 H	4 TO 6	–

SHEET PAN RACLETTE

This recipe caused quite a stir in the test kitchen during development. I'm a traditionalist when it comes to raclette, which for me means potatoes with lots—and lots—of cheese. The team wanted to push the boundaries of this dish further by adding carrots and, as you can see in the recipe below, they won!

2 lb	(900 g) multicolored baby potatoes (white, red and blue), halved
1 lb	(450 g) small Nantes carrots, peeled and halved lengthwise
2 tbsp	(30 ml) olive oil
1 lb	(450 g) raclette cheese, cut into slices 1/4 inch (5 mm) thick, or more to taste
1 tsp	thyme leaves
	Sliced Grison beef, for serving
	Sour gherkins, for serving

With the rack in the middle position, preheat the oven to 425°F (220°C).

On a non-stick sheet pan, combine the potatoes and carrots with the oil. Season with salt and pepper.

Bake for 25 minutes or until the vegetables are tender and golden, stirring halfway through.

Arrange the cheese slices in three rows over the vegetables. Sprinkle with the thyme. Bake for another 3 to 5 minutes or until the cheese has melted. Season with pepper and serve immediately. Serve with sliced Grison beef and sour gherkins.

PREPARATION	COOKING	SERVINGS	FREEZES
20 MIN	30 MIN	8 APPETIZERS OR 4 SIDE DISHES	–

FOR WHEN YOU
FORGOT WHERE YOU PUT
THE RACLETTE SET.

GNOCCHI CARBONARA

2 1/4 cups	(160 g) freshly grated Parmesan cheese
3/4 cup	(180 ml) water
2 packages	(3/4 lb/340 g each) fresh or vacuum-sealed gnocchi
6 oz	(170 g) diced pancetta
2	onions, thinly sliced
3 tbsp	(45 ml) olive oil
1 1/2 cups	(225 g) frozen green peas, thawed
4	egg yolks

With the rack in the middle position, preheat the oven to 425°F (220°C).

In a bowl, combine the cheese and water.

On a non-stick sheet pan, combine the gnocchi, pancetta, onions and oil. Bake for 20 minutes, stirring halfway through, or until the pancetta and gnocchi are golden and crispy. Add the cheese mixture and the peas. Mix well. Bake for another 2 minutes or until the cheese has melted. Remove from the oven. Season generously with pepper. No need to add any salt since the pancetta and cheese are already quite salty.

Serve in warmed shallow bowls. Make a well in the center of each portion of gnocchi and place an egg yolk in each one. Season the egg with pepper and serve immediately.

PREPARATION	COOKING	SERVINGS	FREEZES
15 MIN	22 MIN	4	–

YOU DON'T
EVEN HAVE TO
BOIL WATER!

tomato-cheese
pizza

TOMATO-CHEESE PIZZA

PIZZA DOUGH

3 tbsp	(45 ml) olive oil
3 cups	(450 g) unbleached all-purpose flour
1 tbsp	sugar
1 tbsp	instant yeast
1 1/2 tsp	salt
1 1/2 cups	(375 ml) warm water

TOPPINGS

1 can	(14 oz/398 ml) diced plum tomatoes
1/4 cup	(60 ml) tomato paste
1 tsp	(5 ml) balsamic vinegar
1 tsp	dried oregano
1	garlic clove, finely chopped
2	balls (4 oz/115 g each) mozzarella di bufala, torn and patted dry
	Basil leaves, to taste

PIZZA DOUGH

Lightly oil a sheet pan and line with parchment paper, letting it hang over two sides. Spread half of the oil (1 1/2 tbsp/22.5 ml) over the paper.

In a large bowl, using a wooden spoon, or in a stand mixer fitted with the dough hook, combine the flour, sugar, yeast and salt. Add the water and mix just until the dough starts to form a ball. On a floured work surface, or in the stand mixer, knead the dough for 5 minutes or until smooth. Add a little more flour if the dough is sticky.

Place the dough on the sheet pan. Using a pastry brush, cover the dough with the remaining oil. Using your hands, gently spread the dough out (it should not cover the entire surface of the sheet pan). Cover with a second, inverted sheet pan or plastic wrap. Let rise in a warm spot for 1 hour 30 minutes or until doubled in volume.

TOPPINGS

Meanwhile, in a bowl, crush the tomatoes with a potato masher. Add the tomato paste, vinegar, oregano and garlic. Mix well. Season with salt and pepper.

With the rack in the middle position, preheat the oven to 450°F (230°C).

Using your fingers, press the dough out to cover the entire surface of the sheet pan, leaving some small finger imprints in the dough. Cover with the tomato sauce and cheese.

Bake for 20 minutes or until the bottom of the crust is nicely golden.

Garnish with basil leaves. Delicious served hot or at room temperature.

NOTE *You can completely omit the cheese or add it to only half of the pizza.*

PREPARATION	RISING	COOKING	SERVINGS	FREEZES
25 MIN	1 H 30	20 MIN	6 TO 8	YES

A PIZZA DOUGH DESIGNED TO COOK ON A SHEET PAN.

CHICKEN WITH GRAPES AND CELERY

1	whole chicken (about 4 lb/1.8 kg)
1 tbsp	coarse salt
2 tsp	curry powder
2	garlic cloves, finely chopped
1	lemon, halved
	Olive oil, for cooking
8	stalks celery, cut into pieces
2 cups	(350 g) small seedless red grapes

With the rack in the middle position, preheat the oven to 400°F (200°C).

On a work surface, using a chef's knife or kitchen scissors, remove the backbone from the chicken and open it flat.

Sprinkle the salt, curry powder and garlic over the chicken skin. Rub the spice-covered skin and the inside of the chicken with half of the lemon for 3 minutes. Let rest for 15 minutes. Oil the chicken and season with pepper. Place it flat, skin-side up, on a non-stick sheet pan. Bake for 30 minutes.

Remove from the oven. Arrange the celery, grapes and remaining lemon half cut into wedges around the chicken. Bake for another 35 minutes or until a thermometer inserted in the thigh, without touching bone, reads 180°F (82°C).

Let sit for 5 minutes. Serve the chicken with the celery and grapes. Drizzle with the cooking juices. Serve with quinoa, rice or potatoes, if desired.

PREPARATION	RESTING	COOKING	SERVINGS	FREEZES
15 MIN	15 MIN	1 H 5 MIN	4	−

THE BUTTERFLY TECHNIQUE—THE BEST WAY TO COOK A WHOLE CHICKEN ON A SHEET PAN!

paella

PAELLA

CHICKEN

1 lb	(450 g) boneless, skinless chicken thighs, cubed
1	red bell pepper, seeded and cut into large dice
1	onion, diced
2	garlic cloves, chopped
2 tbsp	(30 ml) olive oil
1 tbsp	(15 ml) tomato paste
2 tsp	sweet smoked paprika
1 tsp	salt

RICE

3 cups	(750 ml) chicken broth
1 cup	(250 ml) dry white wine
1/4 tsp	saffron
1 1/2 cups	(330 g) paella rice, rinsed and drained
1 1/2 cups	(225 g) frozen green peas

SHRIMP

3/4 lb	(340 g) raw medium shrimp (20–40), shelled and deveined
1 tbsp	(15 ml) olive oil
	Lemon wedges, for serving

CHICKEN

With the rack in the middle position, preheat the oven to 425°F (220°C).

In a bowl, combine all of the ingredients. Season with pepper. Spread out on a non-stick sheet pan. Bake for 15 minutes or until the chicken is starting to brown.

RICE

Meanwhile, in a large pot, bring the broth, wine and saffron to a boil. Add the rice. Season with salt. Simmer over medium-low heat for 15 minutes or until the rice is al dente and has absorbed almost all of the liquid, stirring often.

Toss the rice with the chicken on the sheet pan. Using a spatula, spread out in an even layer. Top with the green peas.

SHRIMP

In another bowl, toss the shrimp with the oil. Season with salt and pepper. Spread over the rice on the sheet pan.

Bake for 10 minutes or until the shrimp are cooked through. Garnish with lemon wedges. Serve immediately.

PREPARATION	COOKING	SERVINGS	FREEZES
30 MIN	25 MIN	6	–

NO NEED TO STIR THE RICE. SHOCKING, RIGHT? (WE APOLOGIZE IN ADVANCE TO THE PURISTS!)

RACK OF PORK LOIN WITH ROASTED SHALLOT DRESSING

PORK AND POTATOES

2 lb	(900 g) yellow-fleshed potatoes, unpeeled, each cut into 8 long wedges
3 tbsp	(45 ml) olive oil
1 tsp	black peppercorns
1/2 tsp	fennel seeds
1/2 tsp	red pepper flakes
1 tbsp	finely chopped sage leaves
1/2 tsp	salt
1	rack pork loin (4 bones) (about 2 lb/900 g), trimmed

ROASTED SHALLOT DRESSING

2	shallots, thinly sliced
1/4 cup	(60 ml) olive oil
1 tbsp	(15 ml) balsamic vinegar
1 tsp	(5 ml) Worcestershire sauce

PORK AND POTATOES

With the rack in the middle position, preheat the oven to 425°F (220°C). Line a sheet pan with parchment paper or a silicone mat.

On the sheet pan, toss the potatoes with 2 tbsp (30 ml) of the oil. Season with salt and pepper. Arrange the potatoes around the edges of the sheet pan, away from the center.

Using a mortar and pestle, crush the peppercorns, fennel seeds and red pepper flakes. Add the sage and salt. Mix well. Spread the spice mixture out on a plate. Brush the rack of pork with the remaining oil. Press the pork into the spice mixture and coat well. Place the pork in the center of the sheet pan.

Bake for 25 minutes. Reduce the oven temperature to 350°F (180°C). Bake for another 15 to 20 minutes or until a thermometer inserted in the center of the roast reads 135°F (57°C). Let rest for 10 minutes before slicing.

ROASTED SHALLOT DRESSING

Meanwhile, in a small skillet over medium-high heat, cook the shallots in half of the oil (2 tbsp/30 ml) for 3 minutes or until golden. Pour into a bowl. Add the remaining ingredients and oil. Season with salt and pepper.

Cut the rack of pork between the bones. Serve with the potatoes and roasted shallot dressing, and a green vegetable and fried sage leaves, if desired.

PREPARATION	COOKING	SERVINGS	FREEZES
20 MIN	40 MIN	4	–

SHEET PAN SALMON:
A TRIED-AND-TRUE CLASSIC!

TERIYAKI SALMON FILLET

TERIYAKI SAUCE

1/4 cup	(60 ml) reduced-sodium soy sauce
2 tbsp	brown sugar
1 tbsp	(15 ml) mirin
1 tbsp	cornstarch
1 tbsp	finely chopped fresh ginger
2	garlic cloves, finely chopped
4	green onions, thinly sliced

SALMON AND NAPA CABBAGE

8 cups	(680 g) napa cabbage, cut into slices 1/2 inch (1 cm) thick
2 tbsp	(30 ml) toasted sesame oil
1 1/2 lb	(675 g) salmon fillet with skin

With the rack in the middle position, preheat the oven to 425°F (220°C).

TERIYAKI SAUCE

In a small pot, off the heat, whisk together the soy sauce, brown sugar, mirin and cornstarch. Bring to a boil while stirring constantly. Remove from the heat. Add the ginger, garlic and half of the green onions. Let cool.

SALMON AND NAPA CABBAGE

On a non-stick sheet pan, toss the cabbage with the sesame oil. Season with salt and pepper. Spread out evenly on the sheet pan. Place the salmon on the cabbage, skin-side down. Brush the entire surface of the fish with the teriyaki sauce.

Bake for 15 to 18 minutes or until the salmon is cooked but still pink in the center. Sprinkle with the remaining green onions.

PREPARATION	COOKING	SERVINGS	FREEZES
20 MIN	20 MIN	4	–

perfectly broiled
striploin steaks

roasted mushrooms and asparagus with chive cream

PERFECTLY BROILED STRIPLOIN STEAKS

2 tbsp	milk powder
1 tbsp	unbleached all-purpose flour
1 tbsp	Montreal steak spice
2	beef striploin steaks (each about 1 1/2 inches/4 cm thick), at room temperature for 30 minutes
2 tbsp	(30 ml) olive oil

With the rack in the top third of the oven, preheat a convection oven to broil (see note). Oil a non-stick sheet pan.

In a small bowl, combine the milk powder, flour and steak spice. Place the steaks on a large plate. Lightly season with salt. Sprinkle with the milk powder mixture on both sides (see note). Place on the sheet pan. Coat the steaks with the oil.

Broil for 5 minutes, flip the steaks over and cook for another 5 minutes. Set aside on a plate, cover with foil and let rest for 5 minutes. On a work surface, slice the steaks.

Serve with roasted mushrooms and asparagus with chive cream (recipe opposite) or roasted squash with ricotta (recipe p. 130), if desired.

NOTES *Cooking the steak on convection helps any liquid evaporate and promotes caramelization. Cooking in a traditional oven is possible, but the caramelization of the meat won't be at its best.*

The milk powder and flour help to caramelize the meat.

PREPARATION	COOKING	SERVINGS	FREEZES
10 MIN	10 MIN	4	–

A SHEET PAN STEAK?
A DEFINITE YES FOR EVEN COOKING.

ROASTED MUSHROOMS AND ASPARAGUS WITH CHIVE CREAM

ROASTED MUSHROOMS AND ASPARAGUS

2 tbsp	butter, softened, plus more to taste
1/2 lb	(225 g) white mushrooms, kept whole
8	king oyster mushrooms, halved lengthwise (see note)
3/4 lb	(340 g) small asparagus, trimmed
3 1/2 oz	(100 g) enoki mushrooms, trimmed
1	shallot, chopped
2 tbsp	curly parsley leaves (optional)
1 tbsp	finely chopped tarragon leaves (optional)

CHIVE CREAM

1/2 cup	(125 ml) 35% cream
3/4 cup	(35 g) chopped chives

ROASTED MUSHROOMS AND ASPARAGUS

With the rack in the lowest position, preheat the oven to 450°F (230°C). Brush a non-stick sheet pan with the butter.

Place the white mushrooms and oyster mushrooms, cut-side down, on the sheet pan. Bake for 20 minutes. Add the asparagus, enoki mushrooms and shallot. Season with salt and pepper. Stir gently. Add more butter to taste. Bake for another 5 to 7 minutes, depending on the size of the asparagus.

CHIVE CREAM

Meanwhile, in a small pot, bring the cream and chives to a boil. Season with salt and pepper. In a blender, purée until smooth. Strain through a sieve, if desired.

Serve the chive cream on plates topped with the mushrooms and asparagus. Sprinkle with parsley and tarragon, if desired.

NOTE *King oyster mushrooms can be replaced with a more common type of oyster mushroom or simply by more white mushrooms.*

PREPARATION	COOKING	SERVINGS	FREEZES
20 MIN	25 MIN	4 TO 6 APPETIZERS OR SIDE DISHES	–

PRIME RIB ROAST AND VEGETABLE PAPILLOTE

VEGETABLE PAPILLOTE

12	small carrots, peeled or unpeeled
12	small parsnips, peeled
1	large rutabaga, peeled and cut into 12 wedges
3	onions, peeled and quartered
2 tbsp	(30 ml) olive oil

PRIME RIB ROAST

1 tbsp	unbleached all-purpose flour
2 tsp	crushed black pepper
2 tsp	salt
2 tsp	onion powder
1 tsp	garlic powder
1/4 tsp	ground nutmeg
1	prime rib beef roast (4 ribs) (about 9 lb/4 kg), at room temperature for 1 hour

---

VEGETABLE PAPILLOTE

With the rack in the middle position, preheat the oven to 500°F (260°C).

Layer two large sheets of foil one on top of the other. Place the vegetables in the center of the foil and toss with the oil. Season with salt and pepper. Tightly seal the foil to form a packet (papillote). Set aside.

PRIME RIB ROAST

In a bowl, combine the flour, pepper, salt, onion powder, garlic powder and nutmeg.

On non-stick a sheet pan lined with foil (see note p. 10), rub the roast with the spice mix on all sides. Place the roast, fat-side up, on the sheet pan. Bake for 45 minutes along with the vegetable papillote. After the 45 minutes have passed, turn the oven off, leaving the meat and vegetables inside. Do not open the oven door for 2 hours in order to keep all of the heat inside.

Remove the sheet pan from the oven. Using a chef's knife, separate the meat from the ribs. Thinly slice the meat. Serve with the vegetables, and a Madeira or béarnaise sauce, if desired.

NOTE *For six people, you will only need a 4 1/2 lb (2 kg) roast and half the quantity of vegetables. Cook at 500°F (260°C) for 25 minutes.*

PREPARATION	COOKING	SERVINGS	FREEZES
55 MIN	2 H 45	12	–

THE TECHNIQUE
FOR PRIME RIB
PERFECTION.

BUTTERFLIED BARBECUE CHICKEN WITH CORN

2 tsp	coriander seeds
1 tsp	black peppercorns
1 tbsp	brown sugar
2 tsp	sweet smoked paprika
1 tsp	salt
1/2 tsp	dried oregano
1/4 tsp	cayenne pepper
1	whole chicken (4 lb/1.8 kg)
1 tbsp	(15 ml) vegetable oil
3 tbsp	(45 ml) store-bought barbecue sauce
1 1/2 cups	(225 g) frozen corn kernels, thawed
2	green onions, thinly sliced, for serving
	Thyme leaves, for serving

With the rack in the middle position, preheat the oven to 400°F (200°C).

Using a mortar and pestle, crush the coriander seeds and peppercorns. Add the brown sugar, paprika, salt, oregano and cayenne. Mix well.

On a work surface, using a chef's knife or kitchen scissors, remove the backbone from the chicken and open it flat.

Using a pastry brush, cover the chicken with the oil and sprinkle with the spice mixture. Place the chicken flat, skin-side up, on a non-stick sheet pan.

Bake for 30 minutes. Reduce the oven temperature to 350°F (180°C). Bake for another 30 minutes. Remove the sheet pan from the oven.

Using a pastry brush, cover the chicken skin with the barbecue sauce. Arrange the corn around the chicken on the sheet pan and toss to coat in the cooking juices. Bake for another 10 minutes or until a thermometer inserted in the thigh, without touching bone, reads 180°F (82°C).

Sprinkle with the green onions and thyme leaves. Serve with mashed potatoes, if desired.

PREPARATION	COOKING	SERVINGS	FREEZES
25 MIN	1 H 10	4	–

SPICY CHICKEN WINGS

CHICKEN WINGS

12	chicken wings (see note)
1 tbsp	(15 ml) vegetable oil
1/2 tsp	salt
1/4 tsp	ground black pepper

HOT SAUCE

1	shallot, chopped
3 tbsp	unsalted butter
2 tbsp	(30 ml) spicy piri piri sauce
1 tbsp	sweet paprika
2 tbsp	(30 ml) red wine vinegar

CHICKEN WINGS

With the rack in the middle position, preheat the oven to 425°F (220°C).

On a work surface, cut each chicken wing through the joints into three pieces. Compost or discard the wing tips and keep only the two large pieces of each wing. Pat dry with paper towel.

Place the chicken wings on a non-stick sheet pan. Toss with the oil. Season with the salt and pepper. Arrange in the pan in a single layer.

Bake for 30 minutes or until nicely golden. Remove from the oven. Flip the wings over and bake for another 10 minutes.

HOT SAUCE

Meanwhile, in a small pot over medium-high heat, soften the shallot in the butter. Add the piri piri sauce and paprika. Cook for 1 minute while stirring. Add the vinegar. Simmer for 2 minutes, stirring, or until the sauce thickens. Keep warm while the wings cook.

Pour the sauce into a large bowl. Add the chicken wings and toss well to coat in the sauce.

NOTE *Chicken wings are sold whole or in pieces. If they are whole, you will need to separate them into pieces as described above. Regardless of how you buy them, you will need a total of 24 pieces.*

PREPARATION	COOKING	SERVINGS	FREEZES
20 MIN	40 MIN	4	YES

THIS SHEET PAN
HAS WINGS!

cheese sauce

A SHEET PAN BOOK
WITHOUT A NACHO RECIPE?
NOT ON MY WATCH!

NACHOS

1/2 cup	(65 g) chopped oil-packed pitted black olives
1/4 cup	(40 g) roughly chopped pickled banana pepper rings
1/4 cup	(10 g) finely chopped cilantro
2	green onions, chopped
2 cups	(200 g) grated orange cheddar cheese
2 cups	(200 g) grated mozzarella cheese
1	bag (10 oz/275 g) corn chips
1 1/2 cups	(255 g) diced cooked chicken (see note)
1	recipe cheese sauce (recipe opposite) or 1 cup (250 ml) store-bought nacho cheese sauce
1 cup	(250 ml) sour cream
1 cup	(250 ml) homemade or store-bought guacamole
1 cup	(250 ml) homemade or store-bought salsa
	Lime wedges, for serving

With the rack in the middle position, preheat the oven to 350°F (180°C).

In a bowl, combine the olives, banana peppers, cilantro and green onions. Set aside.

In another bowl, combine the cheddar and mozzarella.

On a non-stick sheet pan, spread out half of the chips. Top with half of the chicken, half of the olive mixture and half of the grated cheese mixture. Repeat with a second layer of chips, chicken, olive mixture and cheese.

Bake for 8 minutes or until the cheese has completely melted.

Serve immediately topped with the cheese sauce, sour cream, guacamole, salsa and garnished with lime wedges.

NOTE *The chicken can be replaced with the same quantity of cooked ground beef.*

PREPARATION	COOKING	SERVINGS	FREEZES
25 MIN	8 MIN	4 TO 6	–

CHEESE SAUCE

1/2 tsp   cornstarch
1/2 cup   (125 ml) milk
1 tbsp   butter
1 tbsp   unbleached all-purpose flour
1/2 tsp   chili powder
1 cup   (100 g) grated sharp orange cheddar cheese

In a small bowl, dissolve the cornstarch in the milk.

In a small pot over medium heat, melt the butter with the flour and chili powder, stirring with a whisk. Cook for 1 minute. Add the milk mixture while whisking. Bring to a boil over medium heat, stirring constantly. Add the cheese and mix until melted. Adjust the seasoning.

This recipe doubles easily. You can make it in advance and store it for 2 weeks in an airtight container in the refrigerator. Warm over low heat before serving.

NOTE *This sauce is also delicious served with burgers.*

PREPARATION	COOKING	MAKES	FREEZES
5 MIN	7 MIN	1 CUP (250 ML), APPROX.	–

SHEET PAN
SWEETS

*A sheet pan dessert never falls flat!
Plus, it travels well.*

chocolate cake
with mousseline cream

FRANGIPANE
AND PEAR TART

1 lb	(450 g) puff pastry, thawed
7 oz	(200 g) almond paste, cut into pieces (see note)
1	egg
2 tbsp	(30 ml) 35% cream
2	firm pears, thinly sliced on a mandoline
3 tbsp	(45 ml) maple syrup

With the rack in the lowest position, preheat the oven to 400°F (200°C). Line a sheet pan with parchment paper.

On a lightly floured work surface, roll out the puff pastry to a 16 × 11-inch (40 × 28 cm) rectangle. Place on the sheet pan. Refrigerate for 15 minutes while you prepare the filling.

In a food processor, finely chop the almond paste. Add the egg and cream. Purée for 1 minute until smooth. Use a spatula to scrape down the sides of the food processor as needed.

Using an offset spatula, spread the almond mixture over the puff pastry. Top with the sliced pears. Using a pastry brush, cover the surface with the maple syrup.

Bake for 25 to 30 minutes or until the crust is slightly golden. Let cool. The tart will keep for 3 days in the refrigerator.

NOTE *There are two types of almond paste. An almond paste with a higher percentage of almonds (between 45% and 52%) is less sweet and works better for recipes like this one, where the paste needs to be creamed or puréed.*

PREPARATION	CHILLING	COOKING	SERVINGS	FREEZES
20 MIN	15 MIN	25 MIN	8	–

PUFF PASTRY + FRANGIPANE + PEARS
= SIMPLE AND SENSATIONAL.

berry pie

BERRY PIE

CRUST
3 cups	(450 g) unbleached all-purpose flour
1/2 tsp	salt
1 cup	(225 g) cold unsalted butter, cubed
1/2 cup	(125 ml) plain yogurt
1/4 cup	(60 ml) ice water

FILLING
1 cup	(210 g) sugar
1/4 cup	(35 g) cornstarch
2 tbsp	instant tapioca
2 tbsp	(30 ml) lemon juice
4 cups	(560 g) frozen strawberries
4 cups	(560 g) frozen blueberries
2 cups	(250 g) frozen raspberries

CRUST

In a food processor, combine the flour and salt. Add the butter and pulse a few times until it forms pea-sized pieces. Add the yogurt and water. Pulse just until the dough starts coming together. Add more water as needed. Remove from the food processor and form into two rectangles with your hands.

On a floured work surface, roll out each portion of dough into a 15 × 12-inch (38 × 30 cm) rectangle. Line a small 13 × 9-inch (33 × 23 cm) sheet pan with one rectangle of dough. Place the other rectangle of dough on a sheet pan lined with parchment paper. Cut into long strips 1/2 inch (1 cm) wide. Refrigerate both sheets of dough for 30 minutes.

With the rack in the lowest position, preheat the oven to 400°F (200°C).

FILLING

In a pot, off the heat, combine the sugar, cornstarch and tapioca. Add the lemon juice and then the strawberries. Bring to a boil. Remove from the heat. Add the blueberries and raspberries.

Spread the berry filling over the dough in the small sheet pan. Place the strips of dough over the filling, weaving them to form a lattice. Trim any excess dough. Press the edges of the dough to seal the layers together. Fold the edges so that they are inside the sheet pan and do not overflow onto the rim. Cover the pie with foil.

Bake for 10 minutes. Remove the foil. Bake for another 35 minutes or until the crust is golden and the filling is boiling. Let cool. The pie will keep for 3 days in the refrigerator. Let sit at room temperature for 30 minutes before serving.

PREPARATION	CHILLING	COOKING	SERVINGS	FREEZES
35 MIN	30 MIN	55 MIN	12 TO 16	YES

JOS LOUIS™
SQUARES!

chocolate cake
and mousseline cream

CHOCOLATE CAKE
WITH MOUSSELINE CREAM

CHOCOLATE CAKE

2 1/4 cups	(340 g) unbleached all-purpose flour
2 tsp	baking powder
1/2 tsp	baking soda
1/4 cup	(25 g) cocoa powder
3 tbsp	(45 ml) hot water
2 tsp	(10 ml) apple cider vinegar
3/4 cup	(170 g) unsalted butter, softened
1 1/2 cups	(315 g) sugar
3	eggs
1 cup	(250 ml) buttermilk

MOUSSELINE CREAM (SEE NOTE)

2/3 cup	(85 g) icing sugar
1 tbsp	unbleached all-purpose flour
1	egg yolk
1/2 cup	(125 ml) milk, warmed
2/3 cup	(150 g) unsalted butter, cubed and softened
4 oz	(115 g) white chocolate, melted and cooled

GANACHE

8 oz	(225 g) dark chocolate, chopped
3/4 cup	(180 ml) 35% cream

CHOCOLATE CAKE

With the rack in the middle position, preheat the oven to 350°F (180°C). Butter a sheet pan and line with parchment paper, letting it hang over two sides.

In a bowl, combine the flour, baking powder and baking soda. Set aside.

In another bowl, combine the cocoa powder, water and vinegar. Set aside.

In a third bowl, cream the butter and sugar with an electric mixer. Add the eggs, one at a time, and whisk until smooth.

With the machine running on low speed, add the cocoa mixture. Add the dry ingredients, alternating with the buttermilk. Spread the batter out evenly on the sheet pan.

Bake for 20 minutes or until a toothpick inserted in the center of the cake comes out clean. Let cool. Unmold. Let cool completely on a wire rack, about 2 hours.

WHITE CHOCOLATE MOUSSELINE CREAM

Meanwhile, in a small pot, off the heat, combine 2 tbsp of the icing sugar with the flour. Add the egg yolk and whisk until smooth.

Gradually whisk in the warm milk. Bring to a boil over medium heat, whisking constantly and scraping the bottom and sides of the pot. Simmer for 2 minutes over low heat. Transfer the pastry cream to a bowl.

Cover with plastic wrap directly on the surface of the pastry cream. Let cool and refrigerate for 1 hour 30 minutes or until completely chilled.

GANACHE

Meanwhile, place the dark chocolate in a bowl.

In a small pot, bring the cream to a boil. Pour over the chocolate. Let sit for 2 minutes without stirring.

Whisk until the ganache is smooth and creamy. Let cool at room temperature until slightly thickened, about 1 hour.

ASSEMBLY

Add the remaining icing sugar to the chilled pastry cream and whisk with an electric mixer until smooth. Add the butter, one or two cubes at a time, whisking constantly until smooth and creamy. Drizzle in the cooled white chocolate while whisking.

Cut off the rounded top of the cake to make it flat, if necessary.

Cut the cake in half crosswise to get two rectangles of equal size.

Gently place one rectangle of cake on a large plate. Spread with the mousseline cream. Top with the second rectangle of cake, flat-side up. Pour the ganache over the cake, letting it run down the sides.

The cake will keep for 5 days in the refrigerator. Let sit at room temperature for 30 minutes before serving.

NOTE *Mousseline cream is a pastry cream to which butter and other flavorings are added, such as white chocolate in this recipe.*

PREPARATION	COOKING	COOLING	SERVINGS	FREEZES
55 MIN	25 MIN	2 H	24	YES, WITHOUT THE GANACHE

carrot cake

CARROT CAKE

CAKE

1 1/2 cups	(225 g) unbleached all-purpose flour
1 tsp	baking powder
1/2 tsp	ground cinnamon
1/4 tsp	ground nutmeg
1/4 tsp	baking soda
1/4 tsp	salt
3	eggs
1 1/4 cups	(265 g) brown sugar
1/2 cup	(125 ml) canola oil
1/2 cup	(125 ml) orange juice
2 cups	(270 g) peeled and finely grated carrots
1/3 cup	(45 g) currants (optional)

ICING

1 package	(9 oz/250 g) cream cheese, softened
2 tbsp	unsalted butter, softened
2 cups	(260 g) icing sugar

CAKE

With the rack in the middle position, preheat the oven to 350°F (180°C). Line a small 13 × 9-inch (33 × 23 cm) sheet pan with parchment paper, letting it hang over two sides.

In a bowl, combine the flour, baking powder, spices, baking soda and salt. Set aside.

In another bowl, whisk the eggs and 1/2 cup (105 g) of the brown sugar with an electric mixer until the mixture is pale, is tripled in volume and falls from the beaters in a ribbon, about 10 minutes.

In a third bowl, whisk together the oil, orange juice and remaining brown sugar. Add the dry ingredients. Using a spatula, gently fold in the egg mixture. Add the carrots and currants, if using, and mix to combine. Spread the batter out evenly on the sheet pan.

Bake for 35 minutes or until a toothpick inserted in the center of the cake comes out clean. Let cool completely on a wire rack, about 2 hours. Pass a thin blade between the side of the sheet pan and the cake.

ICING

In a bowl, beat the cream cheese and butter with an electric mixer. With the machine running on low speed, gradually add the icing sugar and beat until smooth and creamy.

Spread the icing over the surface of the cake. The cake will keep for 5 days in the refrigerator. Let it reach room temperature before serving.

PREPARATION	COOKING	COOLING	SERVINGS	FREEZES
35 MIN	35 MIN	2 H	12 TO 16	YES

tropical pavlova

TROPICAL PAVLOVA

MERINGUE
1 tbsp	cornstarch
1 tbsp	(15 ml) lemon juice
8	egg whites, at room temperature
1 3/4 cups	(370 g) sugar

FRUIT
2 cups	(370 g) peeled, cored and thinly sliced pineapple
2	mangoes, ripe but firm, peeled and cut into thin strips
1	passion fruit, pulp only
2 tbsp	sugar

TOPPING
2 cups	(500 ml) 35% whipping cream
1/3 cup	(45 g) icing sugar

MERINGUE

With the rack in the middle position, preheat the oven to 275°F (135°C). Line a sheet pan with parchment paper.

In a small bowl, dissolve the cornstarch in the lemon juice. Set aside.

In a bowl, whisk the egg whites with an electric mixer until frothy. Gradually add the sugar, whisking constantly, until firm peaks form. Add the cornstarch mixture.

Using a spatula, form the meringue into a 16 × 11-inch (40 × 28 cm) rectangle on the sheet pan.

Bake for 1 hour 30 minutes or until the meringue is slightly golden. Remove from the oven and let cool completely, about 3 hours. It will collapse slightly as it cools.

FRUIT
In a bowl, combine all of the fruit with the sugar. Let sit for 10 minutes.

TOPPING
In another bowl, whisk the cream and icing sugar until medium-firm peaks form.

ASSEMBLY
Place the meringue on a serving dish. Top with the whipped cream. Garnish with the fruit mixture. Serve the pavlova immediately. The pavlova will keep for 2 days in the refrigerator, but it is best served the same day.

NOTE *The meringue must be baked the day you plan to eat it and garnished right before you serve it.*

PREPARATION	COOKING	COOLING	SERVINGS	FREEZES
40 MIN	1 H 30	3 H	12	–

A GREAT WAY
TO USE UP EGG WHITES
AND IMPRESS YOUR GUESTS!

GIANT CHOCOLATE CHIP COOKIE

1 1/2 cups	(225 g) unbleached all-purpose flour
1/2 tsp	baking soda
1/4 tsp	salt
3/4 cup	(170 g) unsalted butter, softened
1 1/4 cups	(265 g) brown sugar
1	egg
1	egg yolk
6 oz	(170 g) dark chocolate, chopped

With the rack in the middle position, preheat the oven to 375°F (190°C). Butter a small 13 × 9-inch (33 × 23 cm) sheet pan and line with parchment paper, letting it hang over two sides.

In a bowl, combine the flour, baking soda and salt.

In another bowl, cream the butter and brown sugar with a wooden spoon. Add the egg and egg yolk. Mix until smooth. Add the dry ingredients and chocolate. Using a spatula, spread the batter out evenly on the sheet pan.

Bake for 20 minutes or until the cookie is slightly golden but still soft in the center. Let cool completely. Cut into squares. The cookie will keep for 3 days in an airtight container at room temperature.

NOTE *This batter also works well to make individual cookies. Form eight balls, using 2 tbsp of batter for each one, and place on a sheet pan lined with a silicone mat or parchment paper. Bake at 375°F (190°C) for 7 to 9 minutes or until the cookies are slightly golden but still soft in the center. Let cool on the sheet pan. Repeat with the remaining batter. The recipe will yield 24 cookies.*

PREPARATION	COOKING	MAKES	FREEZES
20 MIN	20 MIN	12 COOKIES	YES

ONE RECIPE,
TWO WAYS:
TWO DOZEN, OR ONE
GIANT COOKIE.

A CLASSIC
CROWD-PLEASER.

CLASSIC BROWNIES

8 oz	(225 g) dark chocolate, chopped
3/4 cup	(170 g) unsalted butter, cubed
1 cup	(150 g) unbleached all-purpose flour
1/4 cup	(25 g) cocoa powder
4	eggs
1 3/4 cups	(370 g) brown sugar
1/4 tsp	salt

With the rack in the middle position, preheat the oven to 350°F (180°C). Butter a small 13 × 9-inch (33 × 23 cm) sheet pan and line with parchment paper, letting it hang over two sides.

In a bowl, over a double boiler or in a microwave oven, melt half of the chocolate (4 oz/115 g) with the butter. Let cool. Set aside.

In another bowl, combine the flour and cocoa powder.

In a third bowl, whisk together the eggs, brown sugar and salt until smooth. Add the melted chocolate mixture, then the dry ingredients. Mix until smooth. Add the remaining chopped chocolate. Spread the batter out evenly on the sheet pan.

Bake for 20 to 25 minutes or until a toothpick inserted in the center of the brownie comes out with a few crumbs still attached and not completely clean.

Let cool on the sheet pan for 2 hours. Unmold. Cut into squares or diamonds. Serve warm or cold. The brownies will keep for 5 days at room temperature.

PREPARATION	COOKING	SERVINGS	FREEZES
20 MIN	20 MIN	24	YES

strawberry shortcake

STRAWBERRY SHORTCAKE

CAKE

1 cup	(150 g) unbleached all-purpose flour
1 tsp	baking powder
1/4 tsp	salt
6	eggs
3/4 cup	(160 g) sugar

STRAWBERRIES

6 cups	(810 g) quartered strawberries
2 tbsp	sugar
1 tbsp	(15 ml) orange liqueur (optional)
	Thai basil leaves, for serving

WHIPPED CREAM

2 1/2 cups	(625 ml) 35% cream
1/2 cup	(105 g) sugar

CAKE

With the rack in the middle position, preheat the oven to 350°F (180°C). Line the bottom of a sheet pan with parchment paper, letting it hang over two sides. Butter the paper and sides of the sheet pan.

In a bowl, combine the flour, baking powder and salt. Set aside.

In a large bowl, whisk the eggs and sugar with an electric mixer until the mixture is pale, is tripled in volume and falls from the beaters in a ribbon, about 10 minutes.

Sift the dry ingredients over the egg mixture and fold in with a whisk. Spread the batter out evenly on the sheet pan.

Bake for 18 to 22 minutes or until a toothpick inserted in the center comes out clean. Let cool completely on a wire rack, about 1 hour.

STRAWBERRIES
Meanwhile, in a bowl, combine the strawberries with the sugar and orange liqueur, if using. Let macerate for 15 minutes. Drain the strawberries, keeping the syrup.

WHIPPED CREAM
In a bowl, whisk the cream and sugar with an electric mixer until medium-firm peaks form.

ASSEMBLY
Drizzle the cake with the strawberry syrup. Cover with the whipped cream and strawberries. Garnish with Thai basil leaves. The cake will keep for 2 days in the refrigerator.

PREPARATION	COOKING	COOLING	MACERATING	SERVINGS
40 MIN	18 MIN	1 H	15 MIN	16

IT'S IMPOSSIBLE TO MESS UP THIS
SINGLE-LAYER CAKE. WE PROMISE.

A BIG FAVORITE
IN OUR HOME.

giant ice cream
sandwich

GIANT ICE CREAM SANDWICH

1/2 cup	(75 g) unbleached all-purpose flour
1/2 tsp	baking soda
1 oz	(30 g) dark chocolate, chopped
1/4 cup	(55 g) unsalted butter
1/4 cup	(25 g) cocoa powder
3	eggs
1/2 cup	(105 g) brown sugar
1	block (8 cups/2 L) vanilla ice cream

With the rack in the middle position, preheat the oven to 400°F (200°C). Line a sheet pan with parchment paper, letting it hang over two sides. Butter and flour the other two sides of the sheet.

In a bowl, combine the flour and baking soda. Set aside.

In a small pot, melt the chocolate with the butter and cocoa powder. Mix until smooth.

In another bowl, whisk the eggs and brown sugar with an electric mixer until the mixture is pale and tripled in volume, about 5 minutes. With the machine running on low speed, add the dry ingredients. Using a spatula, gently fold in the chocolate mixture. Spread the batter out evenly on the sheet pan.

Bake for 5 minutes or until a toothpick inserted in the center of the cake comes out clean. Let cool for 5 minutes. Unmold. Place the cake on a wire rack and remove the parchment paper. Let cool completely, about 1 hour.

Cut the cake in half crosswise to get two rectangles of equal size.

Cut the block of ice cream in half horizontally.

Place the two pieces of ice cream side by side on one of the cake rectangles and top with the other rectangle, nice-side up. Using a knife, cut the sides of the cakes to make them straight.

Cover and freeze for at least 30 minutes. You can impress 12 guests by serving the sandwich whole in the center of the table. Or you can cut it into 12 smaller sandwiches. Cover each sandwich individually in plastic wrap and keep frozen until ready to serve. The sandwich will keep for 1 month in the freezer.

NOTE *As a special treat for the kids, you can press the sides of the sandwiches into chocolate or multicolored sprinkles.*

PREPARATION	**COOKING**	**COOLING**	**FREEZING**	**MAKES**
25 MIN	5 MIN	1 H	30 MIN	12 SANDWICHES

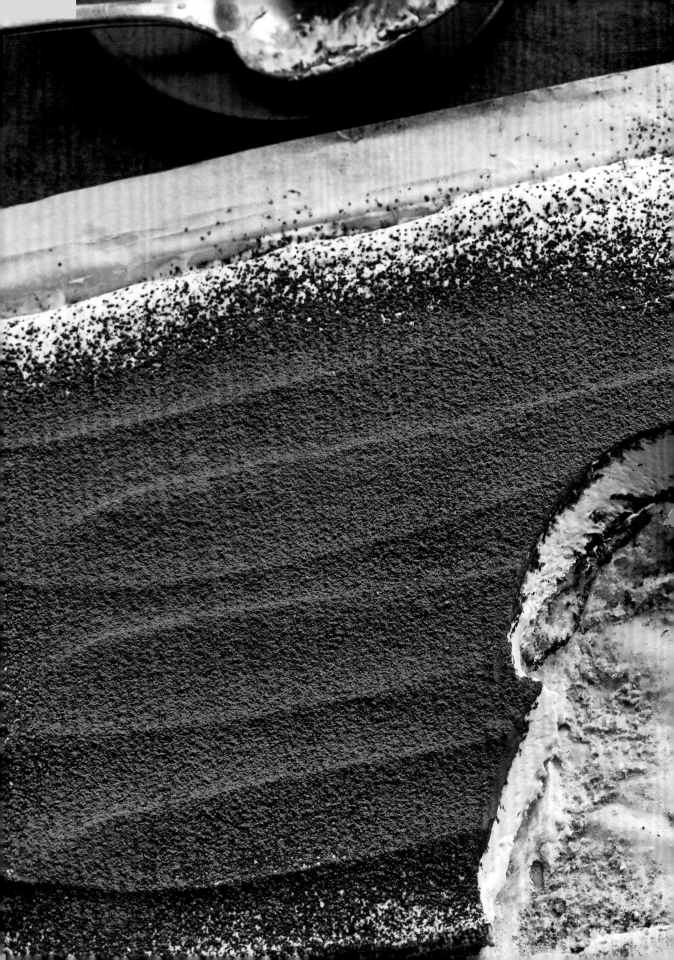

tiramisu cake

TIRAMISU,
IN CAKE FORM.

TIRAMISU CAKE

CAKE

5	eggs, at room temperature, separated
1 cup	(130 g) icing sugar, plus more for sprinkling
1 cup	(150 g) unbleached all-purpose flour

TOPPINGS

1 1/4 cups	(310 ml) hot espresso or strong coffee
1/2 cup	(105 g) sugar
3 tbsp	(45 ml) coffee liqueur
3	egg yolks
1 tsp	(5 ml) vanilla
3/4 lb	(340 g) mascarpone cheese, at room temperature
1 cup	(250 ml) 35% cream
	Cocoa powder, for serving

CAKE

With the rack in the middle position, preheat the oven to 400°F (200°C). Line a small 13 × 9-inch (33 × 23 cm) sheet pan with parchment paper, letting it hang over two sides.

In a bowl, whisk the egg whites with an electric mixer until soft peaks form. Gradually add 1/2 cup (65 g) of the icing sugar and whisk until firm peaks form. Set the meringue aside.

In another bowl, whisk the egg yolks and remaining icing sugar with an electric mixer until the mixture is pale, is tripled in volume and falls from the beaters in a ribbon, about 10 minutes.

Using a spatula, mix one-third of the meringue into the egg yolk mixture, then gently fold in the rest.

Sift the flour over the mixture and gently fold in using a whisk. Spread the batter out evenly on the sheet pan. Sprinkle with a little icing sugar.

Bake for 8 to 10 minutes or until a toothpick inserted in the center of the cake comes out clean and the top of the cake is slightly golden. Let cool completely on a wire rack.

TOPPINGS

In a small bowl, combine the coffee with 3 tbsp of the sugar. Add the coffee liqueur. Refrigerate until ready to assemble the tiramisu.

In a large bowl, whisk the egg yolks, 1/4 cup (55 g) of the sugar and the vanilla with an electric mixer until the mixture is tripled in volume, about 5 minutes.

In another bowl, whisk the mascarpone and remaining sugar (1 tbsp) with an electric mixer until smooth. Add the cream and whisk until firm peaks form. Using a spatula, gently fold the mascarpone mixture into the egg yolk mixture.

Using a pastry brush, cover the cake with the coffee mixture. Top with the mascarpone mixture. Cover with plastic wrap and refrigerate for at least 4 hours or preferably overnight. When ready to serve, sprinkle the cake with cocoa powder. The cake will keep for 2 days in the refrigerator.

PREPARATION	COOKING	CHILLING	SERVINGS	FREEZES
45 MIN	8 MIN	5 H	12	–

THANK YOU!

As I mentioned in the introduction, we started working on this book when the world was a different place. We developed the recipes together (thank you, Etienne, Kareen, Lisa, Nicolas, Danielle), we sampled from each other's plates, we gave each other congratulatory pats on the back.

When it came time to finish the book, we were doing photo shoots with masks on, were taking extreme precautions around each dish and, sadly, had to let go of some of our team members, a disastrous impact of the pandemic. Thank you, Paule, and thank you, Vanessa.

Thanks to my English-language publisher, Robert McCullough, and his team for their trust. It's a pleasure to work with you.

I am surrounded by competent women who know how to adapt despite turmoil. Thank you, Maude B.B., for content direction; Nathalie, for the negotiations and publicity; Maude C., for the incredible photos; Marisol and Eve, organizers extraordinaire for making things happen; and my wife, Brigitte, who absolutely wanted this book to be made for its accessible and unifying aspects.

For the overall look of this beautiful book, thank you to our art director, Cristine; our food stylist, Nataly; our accessories stylist, Sylvain; Geneviève, for graphic design; Jean-Michel, for graphics; and Linda, for computer graphics.

There's been a lot of talk about COVID-19 lately (and often talk only of it). If there is a silver lining among all this tragedy and devastation, it has to be that we all collectively cooked more, for ourselves and our families, and realized that it's something we can all do. The kitchen became a refuge, a positive place for our mental health.

For me, one of the positive aspects of the pandemic has been getting closer to you—you have let me into your kitchens, and your lives, through social media. If there is one way to get more personal, though, it's through this book, touching the paper, taking notes, dog-earing the pages, taking the time to be inspired by the photos. I dedicate this book to all of you who, with resilience, have nurtured those around you with love and good food. Thank you!

Ricardo

INDEX BY SECTIONS

INDEX BY RECIPE TYPE